BLOOD
ON A PEW

BLOOD
ON A PEW

Overcoming Tragedy through
the Truth of Eternity

W. S. Gaines

Tate Publishing & Enterprises

Blood on a Pew
Copyright © 2011 by W. S. Gaines. All rights reserved.

No part of this publication may be reproduced, stored in a retrieval system or transmitted in any way by any means, electronic, mechanical, photocopy, recording or otherwise without the prior permission of the author except as provided by USA copyright law.

Scriptures taken from the *Holy Bible, New International Version*®, NIV®. Copyright © 1973, 1978, 1984 by Biblica, Inc.™ Used by permission of Zondervan. All rights reserved worldwide. www.zondervan.com

The opinions expressed by the author are not necessarily those of Tate Publishing, LLC.

Published by Tate Publishing & Enterprises, LLC
127 E. Trade Center Terrace | Mustang, Oklahoma 73064 USA
1.888.361.9473 | www.tatepublishing.com

Tate Publishing is committed to excellence in the publishing industry. The company reflects the philosophy established by the founders, based on Psalm 68:11,
"The Lord gave the word and great was the company of those who published it."

Book design copyright © 2011 by Tate Publishing, LLC. All rights reserved.
Cover design by Blake Brasor
Interior design by Lindsay B. Behrens

Published in the United States of America

ISBN: 978-1-61777-402-7
1. Biography & Autobiography / Personal Memoirs
2. Religion / Christian Life / Death, Grief, Bereavement
11.08.18

Dedication

To my great-grandmother Myrtle, my grandmother Margie, and my mother, Joyce. The three special women in my life who planted the seed of faith in a small child.

Acknowledgments

I want to thank everyone whom God used to help me put this story on paper. From Randy Testa, a Catholic in Boston, who recognized the significance of the story and sent me an email to nudge me to start writing. His encouragement gave me the confidence to continue writing. To Chris Bean, my neighbor and golf pal, for the many hours spent reviewing and helping tweak the manuscript with an eye that had to come from the Holy Spirit.

I also want to thank Tate Publishing for printing this story for the world to read.

Table of Contents

Foreword 11
Introduction 19
1: The Knock on the Door 23
2: Mercy Hospital 35
3: The Day After 56
4: The Fall 69
Photo Gallery 80
5: Saying Goodbye to a Son 86
6: Football-A Lesson in Life 99
7: Forgiveness 120
8: Moving Forward 133
Bibliography 159

Foreword

It was a simple look.

He was walking out of the University of Pittsburgh weight room when he stopped, looked at me, gave his trademark half-smile, half-smirk and declared, "Yeah, man, I'm back!"

And that was the final time I ever saw number twenty-nine, Billy Gaines.

But it was what led up to that look that made BG the heartfelt competitor he was. He arrived as a five-foot-seven wide receiver from a town that no one could pronounce rocking a grey hooded sweatshirt. It was mid-December, and our position coach and offensive coordinator, JD Brookhart, asked me to host this speedster on his official visit. For thirty bucks and a free dinner, I gladly accepted. After all, how hard could this be?

He arrived at the Hampton Inn with his parents, who had driven the four hours from Ijamsville, Maryland, fresh off a fourth straight high school state championship.

BLOOD on a Pew

Through dinner, this quiet, yet stoic seventeen-year-old kid sat next to me as if no one else was in the restaurant. We talked football, girls, college, and, of course, what it was like to compete with a chip on your shoulder. After all, we were both undersized white receivers on a roster that was dubbed "Wide Receiver University."

As the night continued, we laughed over video games, ate a few trays of Atwood Pizza, and came clean on how we both hated being compared to the famous Notre Dame walk-on, Rudy Ruetigger. "He wasn't even a good player!" we declared in unison.

Billy, or BG as he was now commonly referred to, would eventually sign with Pitt, and our friendship would grow. He would drive to spring practice, watch film, e-mail me with late night questions regarding our offense, and come August, BG was primed for training camp.

BG walked into our first meeting very comfortable. He knew he belonged at this level of competition but also felt that others questioned his ability. After all, he had always had to prove himself.

And during that first practice, he did just that.

Route after route, snap after snap, BG would find himself around the football. If he didn't catch it, he would flash into the screen on the practice film as he raced to throw a block. Yet what was most impressive about the kid who rocked number twenty-nine was when he would get knocked down.

It was like the grass was a springboard. After being tackled or diving for a pass, he would pop up as if it were

Foreword

a competition to get up the quickest. I asked him about why he got up so quickly, and his response was short and stern: "Nothing can keep me down." There was no smile or smirk—BG was straight-faced.

He was on a mission.

Towards the end of his freshman season, BG broke his foot. Devastating to him, he took it in relative stride, but like any freshman, this first year was challenging. He was no longer in the game plans, no longer a focal point during our meetings, and his day consisted of class, rehab on his foot, tutorial sessions, and some down time with his long-time girlfriend, Natalie.

Heading into spring practice, BG was getting healthy, and his itch to perform on the gridiron was apparent. Often, we'd find ourselves sitting outside of study hall at the sandwich shop. BG would be wearing that same grey hoodie, and we'd talk about life and football and how to get through it all. During spring practice he gained confidence, but he also began to consider transferring colleges or changing positions. His passion for the game was fading as his foot injury was holding his game back; I could see this on the practice field and in the weight room. Simply put, Billy had lost his swagger.

Every college football player goes through this funk. You lose confidence, you think of other options, and you forget how much fun the game of football is.

Trust me, I could relate.

So, that summer, after each workout, BG and I began to stay after practice. We'd throw the ball, laugh, and talk route running, secondary coverage's, linebacker recognition, and how the upcoming season would be a blast. Day after day, I'd ask him, "Hey BG, did you have fun today?" And day after day, he'd look at me, smoothly catch my passes, smirk and say, "Nope, not yet." It became a funny little ritual, but with each day, each workout, each throw, and each conversation, BG would have a little more fun and put a little more passion into his game.

It was Tuesday, June 17, when I finally got the answer I'd been waiting for. I can remember we were just leaving our indoor facility on Pittsburgh's South Side when I asked him, "Did you have fun today?" He took a sec, and then said, in his laid-back way, "You know what—today I had a blast. Football was fun again."

Now that was the BG I knew, the BG who led his high school team to fifty straight wins and the BG who ran a 4.22 forty-yard dash in high school, which happened to be a Nike Football Training Camp record. It was the BG who had the ability to start on our team, score touchdowns, become a fan favorite, and someday perhaps even watch his number twenty-nine jersey sell out from the campus bookstore.

He never had that chance.

Around 2:30 the next morning, the unthinkable happened. Billy fell for the last time, and this time he didn't bounce back up. Thirty feet straight down he dropped, hitting his head on a pew. His teammates rushed to his side, called 911, gave him CPR, and prayed that he would regain consciousness. The paramedics arrived, and Billy still had a pulse. Miraculously, he was still with us.

Foreword

Word spread quickly, and early the next morning, I rushed into Coach Brookhart's office where he assured me, "It's serious, but he should be okay." I breathed a sigh of relief and went into the empty team meeting room and sat down next to Larry Fitzgerald, our teammate and All-American wide receiver. Five minutes later, Coach Brookhart stuck his head in the door and said, "It doesn't look good—we should get to the hospital."

"Doesn't look good" didn't register as "might not make it." I mean, how could it? We were Division I athletes; we were invincible. Within hours the whole team had gathered at Mercy Hospital. When we walked in, Billy's entire town was already there, old teammates, family friends, even his pastor. They told us that his hometown was hosting a vigil on Billy's old football field, praying for his recovery. His impact and influence in that room was so strong you could touch it, and it was comforting to know that so many teammates from so many squads were pulling for him. The silences were horrible and awkward, but seeing his parents and his younger brothers, Michael and Nick, was what could rip your heart out. When we hugged in that cold sterile hallway of Mercy Hospital, it was then that I first felt that BG might not live another day.

Amazingly, there were no broken bones, no visible cuts or bruises, but also no brain activity. Billy was gone. After a few hours, we were allowed to see him. I waited and was one of the last people to walk into Billy's room. I think part of it was that I couldn't believe he was not going to make it, and I just wanted someone to walk out and tell me he was talking, laughing, and of course, smirking.

But that wasn't the case. After what felt like a lifetime, I entered the room, I met his grandmother, who asked a few of the players in the room to hold hands and say a prayer together. As we began to follow her lead, I became confused. "Why?" I wondered. I soon understood: It wasn't a prayer that would heal Billy in this life, but a plea to God that would fill us with a peace that could only come from heaven.

It was a prayer of hope.

Then his parents offered me the chance to talk to him, to say good-bye. I nodded, and walked up right next to his bed. There were so many thoughts in my mind, so many questions, and so many things I wanted to say, but nothing of substance came out of my mouth. He looked so peaceful, so happy. He even looked healthy. The previous morning came flooding back to me, when he was smiling, having fun, loving football, loving life. And I wiped my tears, touched his arm, smiled and said, "BG...number twenty-nine...thanks...talk to ya soon, man...love ya."

If there was anybody who hadn't realized it yet, they would find out at his funeral: Billy Gaines was a rock star. His entire school auditorium was full, and they even had to carry the service via satellite into numerous classrooms. Strangely, it didn't feel like a funeral—it felt like a celebration. A celebration of Billy's life, Billy's impact on a small town in Maryland, Billy's ability to change many different communities, and Billy's path. It was epic.

Foreword

His parents were gracious enough to offer the stage to anyone who wanted to speak. Some stories were funny, and some were sad, but all were inspiring. As I sat there with one hundred and four other teammates and our coaching staff, I felt Billy talking to me. "C'mon Yog, tell the story." So I waited until almost everyone had taken a turn, and then I walked what seemed like a mile toward the stage.

I had to tell the story of Billy's last day because no one else knew it. His fans, his teammates, his family, his girlfriend and most importantly his father, who was his best friend, had to hear that Billy left this world a happy man, smiling, laughing, and loving the game that brought so much joy to all of their lives.

I told them how Billy was relentless in his work ethic, thrived in competitive settings, and when he was knocked down during practice, he would bounce up so fast that it looked like the grass was a springboard. And I told them that he was still rocking that old, grey hoodie. I started slowly, but soon the story just flowed as if Billy were right next to me. Now, I'm not the most religious of people, but I do believe that when we pass away from this earth, we also return in some form. Where I always see Billy is in a game somewhere, wearing number twenty-nine and leading a team of football players whose careers on 100 by 53 1/3 yard fields were cut short. There, BG is running routes, watching film, pumping his teammates up, mentoring the new members of his squad, scoring touchdowns, and, of course, competing. That's the only way Billy knew how to do it.

BLOOD on a Pew

My speech wound down and I told the crowd the three sentences that have stuck with me since BG left us: "All heart and he never quit. He hated Rudy, but he loved his last day. All heart and he never quit."

From June 18, 2003, on, every time I walk onto a football field, whether as a player at Pitt, a coach at USC, a broadcaster with Fox or ESPN, or just a fan of the game, the first thing I do is walk to the twenty-nine-yard line, put my toes on it, bend down, line up all ten fingers as if I'm catching a pass from BG, and repeat those words while seeing BG walk out of the University of Pittsburgh weight room, stop, look back, and give his trademark half-smile, half-smirk while declaring, "Yeah, man, I'm back!"

And then I'd smile a half-smile, half-smirk. Just like BG.

— Yogi Roth,
New York Times best-selling author

Introduction

> Always be prepared to give an answer to everyone who asks you to give the reason for the hope that you have.
>
> 1 Peter 3:15

I was telling a couple of friends my plans of writing when I was interrupted with a question.

"Bill, why are you writing the story?"

I was caught off guard by the question, really.

I shouldn't have been. I knew why he was asking. *What was my true motive?* I should have been prepared to answer the simple question, but I found the question challenging.

Why *did* I write this story?

On June 18, 2003, at 2:30 in the morning, my eldest son, Billy, fell through the tile ceiling of a church, crashing into a hard, wooden pew thirty feet below. At the time, he was temporarily staying in the shuttered convent of this Catholic Church, located just outside Pittsburgh, and was attending a late-night party in the church rectory with a few of his University of Pittsburgh football teammates and the parish priest. The priest hosted the event and provided the alcohol. Every one of the football players in attendance, including my son, was underage.

Tragically, later the same day, my son Billy was pronounced brain dead at Mercy Hospital in Pittsburgh. He was nineteen years old.

Just as I was unprepared to explain my motive for writing this story, I was completely unprepared for the tragic, bizarre death of my son, who was about to begin his sophomore year at the University of Pittsburgh on a football scholarship. Nothing could have prepared me for what transpired that early morning in that church.

As if this weren't enough, my father died from cancer just three years after burying his grandson. The story continued, and the tug to write became even stronger. Yet life went on, and I found it impossible to put it all down on paper, let alone attempt to make sense of it all. The story took an ugly turn and became even more tragic.

On March 10, 2007, my youngest son, Nick, a senior in high school, left a late night neighborhood party for a 7-Eleven run and got behind the wheel after drinking with his high school pals. On the way back from the 7-Eleven, on a dark, curving road around 4:30 a.m., Nick lost control and crashed his pickup truck into a tree. He survived after weeks in the hospital and several surgeries. But his best friend, Tyler, who was riding in the passenger seat, was killed instantly.

Introduction

Nick would turn twenty in jail, serving a twelve-month sentence. But he would also receive a life sentence of a different sort. Though he has no memory of that fatal night, due to a severe concussion, Nick will never forget the consequences of being behind the wheel and losing control of his truck, causing the death of his beloved friend Tyler, who had just turned sixteen.

When I stood up to address the packed house at my son's funeral six years ago, I was without words. I knew I had something to say, a message to get across, a reason for hope, but I wasn't prepared. I didn't have the words to explain the reason for this undeniable hope.

When I stepped down from the stage on that dreadful day, I knew something else was missing. I had a strong sense of an unfinished mission. I knew I had to turn the mission over to God and trust Him to communicate and complete the message. But how would God use this opportunity?

It was time for me to write.

I wrote this story to share my personal journey through horror, sadness, anger, and grief and how I survived every parent's worst nightmare to awake from that same nightmare to discover God's grace and mercy.

This is not an easy story for me to tell. It will never be an easy story to tell. Maybe that's why it took me over six years to put it down on paper.

My goal in writing this story was to describe how my journey through despair and darkness led me to the foot of the cross. It was Charles Spurgeon, England's best-known preacher for most of the second half of the nineteenth century, who wrote:

The comfort obtained by others may often prove helpful to another, just as wells would be used by those who came after. We read some good book full of consolation. Ah! We think our brother has been there before us and dug this well for us as well as for himself. Travelers have been delighted to see the footprints of a man on a barren shore, and we love to see the waymarks of pilgrims while passing through the vale of tears.

Why *did* I write this story?

I believe the words in 1 Peter 3:15 explain it best. "Always be prepared to give an answer to everyone who asks you to give the reason for the hope that you have."

This story is my way of sharing that hope with you.

I wrote this story as if I were truly writing for an audience of One. I wrote this story as if I were truly sharing it with the world. I wrote this story for the person taking the time to read it. Ultimately, I wrote this story for you.

1: The Knock on the Door

> Call on Me in the day of trouble; I will deliver you, and you shall honor and glorify Me
> Psalm 50:15

It was 4:30 a.m. on Wednesday June 18, 2003, when we heard the barking downstairs. Nala, our ninety-pound black Shepherd-Lab mix, barked at anything that moved near the house, and most of the time, it was a rabbit or cat, but this time, it was different. My wife, Kim, rolled over and said, "Someone's knocking!"

Wide awake now, my heart skipped a beat. "Who is knocking at this hour?" I replied, as if she had any idea. I peeked through the blinds and spotted a car parked out front. "It's the police!" I said in a loud whisper. With three teenage sons, ages fourteen, sixteen, and nineteen, I should have been worried, but I assumed there was a prowler in the neighborhood, and I calmly walked across the bedroom. We grabbed our robes and slowly made our way down the stairs.

We slowly open the front door. "Do you have a son attending the University of Pittsburgh?" the female police officer asked.

Kim replied without hesitation. "Yes, Billy," she said, with that same pride she always had when she mentioned his name.

"Billy was in an accident and is at Mercy Hospital in Pittsburgh," the officer explained. She said the hospital tried calling several times, but couldn't get an answer, so they sent the police.

"Was he in his truck?" Kim asked.

"No," the police officer replied. "He fell through a roof of a church."

I had unplugged the phone next to my bed Sunday afternoon for a Father's Day nap and had forgotten to plug it back in. The officer handed Kim a little piece of paper with the phone number to Mercy Hospital and explained that Billy was still alive but in critical condition. The officer then asked politely, but in a guarded tone, if she could come in while we made the call to the hospital.

That was a red flag; suddenly, I suspected her reason for coming went beyond passing along a phone number. She was here in case we needed help getting through something—something unthinkable.

My eyes were wide open at this point, and my antennae fully extended. I hadn't said a word to this point, and I probably made the police officer a little nervous with

1: The Knock on the Door

my intense stare. My heart was pounding through my robe as I watched the police officer as if she were the ghost of gloom and doom.

I had no idea what to say or think, but I feared the Grim Reaper had made his way to Nicholas Court and had stopped at our front door. Somehow, I knew.

"Would you like to have a seat?" I asked the officer in a shaky voice.

"Thanks," she replied as she sat across from me at the kitchen table. She was watching Kim closely as Kim started to dial the number. I continued to stare across the table, and I began to read the officer's body language and facial expressions. She tried to ignore me, but finally she turned, looked me in the eyes, and asked, "Do you have any other children?"

My jaw dropped. It seemed like an innocent enough question, but it wasn't, and we both knew it.

I heard Kim on the phone, asking the question that was gnawing at me.

"Is he alive?" Kim asked in a hushed voice.

Frozen for what seemed like several seconds, Kim didn't respond. I closed my eyes and held my breath. She told the person from the hospital we would be there in about three hours and hung up the phone quickly.

"He's alive, but not breathing on his own, and he's in serious condition," Kim quivered with tears in her voice.

The police officer seemed relieved that Billy was still alive, and she left her card. We thanked her for making the trip in the middle of the night and walked her to the door.

BLOOD on a Pew

Kim called Billy's girlfriend, Natalie, to give her the bad news and asked if she could spread the word. We planned to pick Natalie up on the way out of Urbana, Maryland.

Kim woke our two other sons—Nicholas, fourteen, and Michael, sixteen—and told them to get ready quickly, as we were headed to Pittsburgh.

"Your brother was in a serious accident and is in the hospital," Kim told them, and that was all they needed to hear. They quickly jumped out of bed, asking very few questions.

I began to go through my normal morning routine, brewing a pot of coffee and grabbing my travel mug, but I never poured the coffee. I turned off the pot and grabbed my jacket instead. I was last out of the house. I jumped into the front passenger seat of our Mercury station wagon, and Kim started to back out of the driveway.

It was still dark outside and very quiet. It was a damp, dreary morning and a little cool for June. Kim drove, as she gets carsick in the passenger seat, and I don't mind being chauffeured one bit.

After just a few minutes, we pulled into Natalie's driveway to find her walking down her front walkway with a sense of urgency to her step. She climbed into the backseat and told us she had called several friends about Billy's accident. Word was spreading quickly.

After twenty minutes, we were driving out Interstate 70 West, headed for the Pennsylvania Turnpike. We seemed to be making good time, as the roads were still dark and empty. The car was quiet, except for the cell

1: The Knock on the Door

phone conversations with family and friends, who were being updated with what little information we had at the time.

Ten minutes later, we received a call from Coach JD Brookhart, Billy's receivers coach at Pittsburgh. He told us the team and the coaching staff were praying for us and that he would meet us at the hospital. He really didn't have anything new about Billy's condition, and that was probably because the hospital was waiting to speak with us first. The conversation was brief, but I appreciated the update.

As we hit the Pennsylvania Turnpike and headed west for Pittsburgh, I tried to stay positive and reminisce on the few football trips Billy and I had taken on this same highway over the past few years.

There were so many exciting memories for a father and son. I thought about that June week we had together in 2001.

Wow, I thought to myself, *it was exactly two years ago.*

In five days, we traveled to Pittsburgh, West Virginia, and Virginia for their summer football camps, and it was like a father-son vacation for us.

I thought about the two Nike camps at Penn State in May of 2000 and 2001. I could remember the official visit to Pittsburgh with his mother joining us in early December 2001 and how excited we all were. I thought about all of the Pitt home games in 2002 and the football banquet in January 2003 and how much we enjoyed that. There was the spring game just a couple of months ago in April 2003, with Billy's friends from his high school making the trip as well.

It was an exciting few years of traveling up and down the turnpike. We were planning on several more, but this trip would be different. This trip would be our last.

As we neared the hospital, I couldn't help but notice the silence in the car. With Michael, Nick, and Natalie in the backseat and Kim driving, I expected to hear some nervous chatter, but it was dead silent.

At one point, the silence was interrupted. Kim just started crying. She turned to me and said something I'll never forget.

"Bill, please tell me that God won't take my baby home."

I tried to stay focused on a happy ending to this early morning scare. So I replied.

"Maybe it's just a scare. Maybe it was just a close call."

Then, I paused and noticed she calmed down a little. I continued.

"All we know so far is Billy is hurt. Maybe he will have to take an injury red shirt year, which means he would get a year to recover without losing a season of eligibility to play football. He could come back bigger and stronger and a year older."

Kim seemed to accept that for now, but that was just my hope, and I quietly prayed for such a scenario. I had no idea what was coming.

But what if Billy was hurt really badly? What if his football career was over? Well, though it would be tough, he could focus on graduating and working in his chosen

1: The Knock on the Door

profession. He's had an incredible football career up to this point, and he can be thankful for his time.

So again, I quietly closed my eyes and prayed. This time, I prayed for time; I prayed for a second chance. I prayed Billy would get a second chance at life.

But the scenario started to get darker, the choices bleaker.

My mind and heart searched the core of my soul for answers. What would life be like taking care of a handicapped son? Trapped in a wheelchair, paralyzed, perhaps even severely brain-damaged? He would be miserable stuck in a chair or bed for a day, nevermind a lifetime. We would suffer watching him endure his days trapped in a broken body, or even worse, a damaged mind. But it was a possibility; it had to be considered.

I thought about the remarkable story of Chucky Mullins, a University of Mississippi football player who was paralyzed in 1989.

He was a nineteen-year-old freshman defensive back who was paralyzed from the neck down while making a tackle in a game.

Chucky Mullins lowered his helmet and buried it into the receiver's back who went airborne to catch a pass. The impact of the hit knocked the ball out for an incomplete pass, but Chucky shattered his neck in the collision, and he never moved again.

Chucky Mullins died May 6, 1991, at Baptist Memorial Hospital in Memphis, Tennessee, from complications of a blood clot in his lungs. He was twenty-one.

His tombstone is marked simply, "Chucky, Man of Courage."

I would learn more about his story as I searched for answers in my own tragic circumstances over the coming months.

I knew no matter what scenario played out, this accident had to have a meaning deeper than I could have ever imagined. My quiet, secure life was about to be disrupted. I was content with my life and felt very blessed up to this point, and now I was driving to the hospital, bracing myself for what would be every parent's worst nightmare.

I had to come to terms with yet another scenario, one I had blocked out, a choice I couldn't fathom. What would life be like without Billy? I couldn't comprehend it. I had to try to prepare for the possibility, but it was too hard to even imagine.

So I prayed again, and this time it was extremely difficult to find the words. I would lean back in my seat and look up with my eyes closed; I would quietly pray.

Lord... then my mind would go blank.

Nothing! How do I pray for something that I can't even comprehend? I had so many thoughts racing through my head, from an injury that could be overcome to death that could destroy us. Where would I find the words to pray? I just prayed I wouldn't have to comprehend. I prayed for life, but my prayer was weak; I felt weak. Physically and spiritually, I felt my body slowly drain. It was like I had my wind knocked out.

I still didn't have the details, and I didn't know Billy's fate, but I felt like this was going to be the beginning of

1: The Knock on the Door

something, not the end. I knew this was going to be the first round of a battle or the birth of a life, not the last chapter or the end of a life.

I could feel myself reenergize as if I were preparing for a fight. This was going to be a test of sorts. I had no idea to what extent or in what way my family and I would react. But a reaction would be unavoidable. If a chapter were about to close, then a new chapter had to begin, because the story wasn't ending here. I still held on to the first scenario that Billy would be okay. I couldn't picture the accident, and when I tried, I visualized him falling from a roof outside of a church onto a soft landing, like clouds. Besides, all we knew at that point was Billy was in serious condition from a fall from a church roof.

Nothing else.

We stopped twice on the way for gas and a bathroom break, and each time, Kim would start conversations with total strangers and ask them to pray for us. We had people praying for us while we drove to the hospital.

My mind tried to protect me as I drifted to Pitt's spring game a couple of months back and how special that game was to us. It was during a time Billy really didn't know where he stood on the team. His spring practices were very uneventful and a little frustrating, as he complained to me a couple of times about not touching the ball and feeling a little ignored by the coaches.

I don't remember what I said, but I provoked a little fire with an e-mail to Billy during spring practices, and this was his e-mail response to me:

BLOOD on a Pew

Thanks for the article. I know where I stand in the eyes of the media and the public, but I also know where I stand in my own mind. So far I feel like an entirely different player in spring ball. It is becoming a game again and not Hell. I am working myself back into shape and I am more sore everyday than I have ever been, but it will all pay off. Strength wise I am still building my legs back up, but my upper body is stronger than it has ever been. I'm not trying to earn anyone's respect but my own. Everyone else's respect I am gonna have to take, so thanks for adding a few more chips to my shoulder. I'll be sure to take care of them all the best way I know how to. Tell everyone I said hey. Talk to ya later, I have practice.

–Billy

I always had a knack for adding a few more "chips" to a set of shoulders that already carried a couple bags. You won't find many undersized football players without their share of doubters. It is a game of giants.

At the spring game breakfast, the new running back coach came up to Billy as we ate and mentioned how strong Billy looked. The funny thing was, when the coach left the table, Billy was shocked the new coach even remembered his name. He thought that might have been the first time the coach ever talked to him.

It was that kind of spring.

But there was one coach who knew his name. The receivers coach, Coach Brookhart, came up and whispered in Billy's ear that Billy would get the ball on a

1: The Knock on the Door

reverse on the first play of the game. Billy was shocked; he didn't get that call once during spring practice, and now, in the spring game, they want to call his number on the first play. He just looked at me and shook his head in disbelief.

Billy went on to have a good game with five receptions, a couple of reverses, and a thirty-nine-yard touchdown catch. After the game, he felt he had earned a little respect from his coaches. He had a little swagger back in his step and was looking forward to competing for some playing time in the fall. Even with the good game and the respect he perceived from some of the coaches, there was always a comment that seemed to follow a compliment. "Obviously, his size is his only drawback," one of the coaches said to the media at the end of his interview about Billy's performance.

He would always be considered an "overachiever," being five-feet-seven and one hundred and seventy-five pounds.

As we were saying good-bye, I hugged him and whispered, "You made us proud today."

I think I caught him off guard, as he looked a little surprised and just grinned and said, "Thanks, Dad."

Little did I realize that would be the last time I hugged my son.

As we passed the Pittsburgh suburb of Oakland and were approaching the exit to Mercy Hospital, the clouds never left us. It was after 8 a.m., and the traffic was heavy with Wednesday morning commuters. I found myself praying again, still struggling to find the words to approach God in prayer, still speechless and dazed.

I asked many questions during this long drive, and it was at this point I asked myself, *Where is God in all this?* As we approached Mercy Hospital that dreary morning, I had to shake that heavy burden that weighed me down and refocus my energy on the reality in front of me. *All that matters now is Billy's health. If Billy survived this accident, I will give God the credit for this miracle,* I thought to myself as we drove through the heavy traffic. What a wonderful inspiration that would be. What a powerful testimony, indeed. *Billy's miraculous recovery—I can see it now.*

Up to that point in my life, I went out of my way to live a safe and secure life of limited stress. I wasn't looking for any trouble. I kept a simple schedule with few outside obligations. I didn't serve in my church and only coached my son's sports teams a few times through the years. I was content being on the sidelines, deep within my comfort zone. Pursuing happiness through avoiding pressure, my intention was to keep my gradual journey to the grave as quiet and safe as possible, arriving safely in a secure and unscratched body without ripples or waves—just floating along in that muddy, shallow water of mediocrity.

I didn't know it at the time, but the hell I was about to experience would force me to wake up, and it would change my life forever. For the first time in my life, I was going to feel totally unprotected by God, and I was confronted with a heavy question; for all those years, as I quietly prayed safety over my children before dozing off for the night, who was it I was praying to?

2: Mercy Hospital

> Do not be afraid of those who kill the body but cannot kill the soul. Rather, be afraid of the One who can destroy both soul and body in hell.
> Matthew 10:28

A little after 8 o'clock, we pulled into the parking lot in front of Mercy Hospital. Kim and I were met by a couple of the football coaches. They were waiting outside, and they started walking towards us as we parked the station wagon. I could see from their demeanor Billy's condition wasn't good. As we were walking into the hospital, one of the coaches gave me a brief update on what he knew about the accident so far. I was told about the party in the church. I was told that alcohol was consumed at the party and that Billy had alcohol in his system when he fell. The coach tried to describe how Billy crawled into the attic space above the sanctuary and slipped through the ceiling, but my head was spinning with questions at that point. I couldn't wrap my mind around it. I couldn't picture it. I just couldn't accept the story. It seemed too bizarre.

Billy and his five roommates had narrowly escaped a fire that burned their row house rental a couple of months ago. I knew they were renting rooms in a church convent until they found another place, but w*hy was he drunk in a church ceiling in the middle of the night?* I couldn't get past that question.

After we got to the front counter, we were told to wait in the lobby area on the ICU floor for the nurses to come by with an update. When we got to the lobby, we were greeted by Billy's teammate, David Abdul, and David's girlfriend, Nicole.

Head Coach Walt Harris was waiting in the lobby also, quietly playing a board game with his young son. I didn't have a conversation with the coach because neither one of us really knew what to say.

The waiting room was quiet in anticipation as we waited for the nurses. David and Nicole were sitting and staring at the wall in shock while Beverly, David's mother, held her infant grandson, Chase. Nobody knew what to say, so we said nothing.

A million questions went through my head as I sat there staring at the brick wall through the large glass window, but I didn't dare ask for fear of getting answers I wasn't ready to accept.

I couldn't believe this was happening. I started to feel sorry for myself. I wanted to hide. I had to change my

2: Mercy Hospital

focus. By the grace of God, I was able to focus on the people around me.

The University of Pittsburgh athletic director and football director came by to show their support. With each person who expressed their concern about Billy and us, I felt myself feeling bad that they had to go through this ordeal as well. In some ways, it helped me cope with the situation. My focus was diverted from my anxiety over Billy's condition to the concern of the people around me.

After about ninety minutes of waiting, we finally stepped out to the hallway and met with two ICU nurses. They had that same look of despair the coaches had. They were choosing their words carefully as they updated us on Billy's condition. I began reading their faces more than hearing their words; their eyes told me everything I needed to know about Billy's condition, and it wasn't good. After explaining the various scans the surgeons were reviewing, they basically told us to wait for the surgeon to give us his prognosis.

At that point, Kim asked, "Is Billy conscious?"

The nurse answered, "No."

"Is he breathing on his own?"

Again, the nurse answered, "No."

They could tell we didn't get it yet.

We were finally allowed to see Billy. We followed the nurses through layers and layers of doors. It seemed like miles of hallways and locked doors.

Kim looked over at me while we were following the nurses through the hallways and said, "Once Grammy gets here and starts praying, there is no way God will say no."

We finally went through the last door and turned left. Billy was in the first bed to the left with just a pull curtain for privacy and a busy counter just a few feet away from his feet.

I felt like he was on display. It felt like we were on display. He was on life support, and he looked like he was sleeping. He looked very peaceful and content, even with the various tubes keeping his body alive. His skin was unscratched, and his body appeared unharmed, but he was hurt bad, as the back of his head had taken the brunt of the blow when he crashed down on the hard, wooden pew some thirty feet below.

Kim, Michael, Nick, Natalie, and I gathered around his bed.

We whispered encouragements to him, looking for any kind of response, but there wasn't any. We told him we were there and that we loved him, but we were uncertain if he heard us at all or if he was even still there. With every twitch of his arm, we all perked up, trying to justify it as a response to a word or a touch, hanging on to the possibility that he heard us.

I began to consider a deeper meaning behind the accident as early as when we received the knock on the door a few hours prior. As a believer, you typically look for God in everything—the good, the bad, and the ugly. But it's in the bad and the ugly that we need Him most and yet He can seem the furthest away.

2: Mercy Hospital

I was asking myself the same questions over and over. *Where is God in all this? Where were You when Billy was in obvious danger? Why didn't You protect him this time? God, where are You now?*

I always felt my family and I were protected by God—a feeling that enabled me to sleep at night, knowing we were being watched over. I began to believe I was naive to trust God. I thought I lived in reality, but perhaps I was living in a fantasy.

My son fell to his death in a church and smashed the back of his head against a wooden pew. My son bled on a church pew and the blow to his head killed him. He died in a church. There is no pleasant way to describe it. It's the cold hard fact. This horrific tragedy had to mean something, didn't it? There must be a deeper meaning behind this bizarre accident. What did this mean to my family and me? Why was Billy the one? Why was he the one who had to die? What was the deeper message, and who was sending it? How should I react to this unthinkable tragedy? And perhaps the most significant question of all, how does God want me to respond?

During Billy's freshman year of college, he was in the process of choosing a second tattoo. He had the cross with barbed wire going through it on his left bicep, and now he was ready for another tattoo—something he would burn into his skin and carry on his body for the rest of his life, something with meaning and purpose.

He wanted a verse from the Bible, and he asked me if I had any suggestions. Without hesitation, I told him about a verse I had heard recently while listening to

BLOOD on a Pew

James Earl Jones read the Bible on tape while I was driving to work. It stopped me in my tracks, and I hit rewind a couple of times until I was sure I had heard it right. I went home and read the passage a couple of times to be sure I had the correct interpretation. It was a verse of courage. It was a verse that described an attitude. This was a verse that wrapped you in a protection that can only come from God. It was a verse for a warrior.

I told Billy that it was in Matthew, but that I wasn't sure where. It said something like, "Don't fear anything or anybody in this world; only fear God who has control of both your body and soul." He got the point, and it sounded like the verse he was looking for. He set out to find it, but I'm not sure he had time.

The verse was Matthew 10:28: "Jesus says, 'Do not be afraid of those who can kill the body but cannot kill the soul, rather be afraid of the One who can kill both body and soul in Hell.'"

When I heard that verse in my car that afternoon from the deep powerful voice of James Earl Jones, it was as if God Himself was talking directly to me and sending me a message.

It's not about the body—it's all about the soul.

It was a clear warning from heaven that living in this dangerous world, a battleground for our souls, we are open and vulnerable to physical attacks, accidents, and diseases that can harm us even kill us, but not to fear, because it is God who protects our souls in eternity. It is God who has the ultimate power and control, and it is God who has His protective hand over our eternal souls.

2: Mercy Hospital

With the curtain still wide open and several nurses within earshot, the surgeon walked up and introduced himself. He looked to be in his sixties, with a full head of gray hair. He had a slight accent but was easy to understand. He briefly described the results of the various scans of Billy's brainstem and spinal cord, but I waited for the bottom line.

After the doctor went over Billy's scans, each worse than the last, with no brain activity and severe, permanent spinal injuries, the news finally hit.

"Your son is brain dead," the surgeon said.

I heard crying behind me, but it was soft and controlled. I felt numb and dizzy at the same time. I felt shock starting to set in. There was a numbness pouring over my soul that could only come from God's hand, a heavy dose of anesthetic from heaven, an anesthetic that enabled me to survive the emotional and spiritual ripping of my heart from my chest as the cold hard reality set in.

I was receiving this anesthetic as the surgeon spoke. I would need more as the day wore on, as my life wore on.

I felt the intensity of that invisible spotlight from heaven—that same spotlight that followed us from Maryland. *What if this guy is wrong?* The surgeon waited for a response. I didn't accept his diagnosis, and I think the surgeon was surprised by my lack of response.

I looked him in the eye and asked, "Has there ever been a case where someone recovered from this state?"

With a slight nervous grin, the surgeon said, "No! This is what happens when kids drink."

BLOOD on a Pew

I was speechless. I couldn't believe the timing of his insensitive remark.

I glanced over at Kim, and I could tell she was about to explode. I braced myself, as I knew she was about to give the surgeon her opinion on his rather tactless comment. But by the amazing grace of God, she bit her tongue, closed her eyes, and I whispered a little prayer. "Dear God, please put Your arm around her shoulders and Your hand over her mouth."

The surgeon then added, "But two other doctors must confirm your son's death with at least one hour between each diagnosis before your son is considered officially dead." So the surgeon left us with a sliver of hope. I was grateful I didn't need to put Billy's fate in the hands of one fallible doctor.

I'm sure the surgeon's cool demeanor was unintentional, as he probably delivered this kind of dire news on a regular basis. *Maybe this guy is wrong?* We held onto the hope. *Surely, the next surgeon will see life. The next surgeon will have a different answer, and Billy will survive.*

As I watched the surgeon leave, he turned to one of his nurses with what appeared to be a sigh of relief. He was probably thinking, *I'm glad that's over,* as he started down the hall for what was probably a typical day at the hospital for him.

We got a taste of what was far from a typical day for the people who loved Billy. This day was just beginning, and it would prove to be long and brutal.

When we were left with the devastating news, each of us had to grieve in our own way. We had no privacy.

2: Mercy Hospital

There was no privacy from the many people working behind the counter and walking by the curtain as we grieved and no privacy from the less obvious, invisible audience that watched from an unseen curtain that had been pulled wide open for all to see.

Soft crying came from the people around me. My heart began to crumble at the sounds of grief. My heart crumbled from my own grief, but in my mind, I had to get it together. I had to be strong for my family.

My mind drifted from the individual hurt around me to the bigger picture that surrounded my soul. I wasn't focused on the reality that was lying near me in the hospital bed or the grief that would soon swallow me like a whale swallowing a minnow. I was too busy trying to make sense of it all, trying to figure out what it all meant and why it was happening to us.

Nick, our youngest son, so distraught and upset by the news, stormed out into the hallway, almost breaking the swinging door off its hinges. I went out after him, and as soon as I got out to the hallway, my cell phone rang. It was my mother, Billy's grandmother, Grammy, and she was in the passenger seat as my sister Cindy was driving up the Pennsylvania Turnpike from Maryland.

My mother is a spiritual lady who joined the Pentecostal Church when we were teenagers. She strongly believed in the power of prayer and miracles from the hand of God, and this day would be no different. I answered my cell phone, and before I could speak, she said, "I've been praying, and Billy is going to be okay."

They were about thirty minutes away, and I interrupted her before she could say another word. "Mom, he's gone," I muttered in a very weak and broken voice.

Her strong, optimistic voice turned to sobs. "No! No! Billy!"

I heard my sister in the background sobbing.

It was loud and uncontrolled, and it was ripping my shattered heart further. I couldn't believe those words—"Billy is gone"—were actually coming from my mouth, and it was the first time in my life I had heard my mother or sister cry. It was the first time that day I had heard loud sobbing over Billy, and it was killing me inside.

Once again, my pain was diverted to my mother losing her grandson and my sister losing her nephew. I tried to calmly explain to my mom that two more doctors had to test Billy before he would be officially pronounced dead by the hospital and that there was still hope. She sounded like she accepted that, and her tone slowly changed from sorrowful to hopeful by the time we hung up the phone. My mind was racing, and I knew I had to step up to get through the day.

One of the first people to arrive at the hospital was Guy Kneebone, the pastor at an evangelical church we had been attending for several years. I was glad he made the two-hundred mile drive in the predawn hours of the morning. We all needed support, and God was using His people in so many ways. Pastor Guy asked me if he could pray for Billy and for us. He invited anybody who felt compelled to pray to join in. We circled Billy's bed, and

2: Mercy Hospital

we all held hands to pray. As we prayed, my mind drifted, and I quietly began to question God.

I had my own silent prayer, a prayer of questions. I had prayed specifically on many occasions for God to lead Billy to the right school and to protect him. *Is this my answer? Was this the right school? What kind of protection is this?* I knew this wasn't the time to be questioning God, but a time to be pleading with Him. Doubt had clearly chiseled its way back into my soul.

During the prayer, I prayed aloud, something I typically tried to avoid and was uncomfortable with. But the words had to come out; there was no holding them back. The dam had broken, and the words poured out like a waterfall. There wasn't anything captivating or authoritative about the words to my prayer. I was just a terrified father humbly pleading to God for a miracle. The spirit of God was pouring through me, and there was no holding Him back.

I felt weak and humbled as I asked God to bring back my son. I felt inadequate and undeserving to even be making such an enormous request. I referred to Billy as "our gift," when I prayed, completely unaware of Psalm 127:3 at the time. "Behold, children are a gift of the Lord. The fruit of the womb is a reward." The word "gift" was so appropriate; much of what I lived and breathed since Billy's death would come to light weeks, months, and even years later. It would be confirmed and illuminated in God's Holy Scripture.

Our gift had been snatched back, and our reward had been turned into a brutal punishment. I knew it would take a miracle. Billy had already been declared brain-dead, but we prayed for a miracle anyway. I felt weakness and desperation I had never felt before. I felt dependency on God I had never experienced. I knew God had the power to bring Billy back, but was it His will?

Our son was a gift in so many ways. I was slowly accepting the fact that now it appeared God was taking him back, denying us the opportunity to watch him live out his dreams, our dreams for him. I couldn't believe it was actually happening. If God has your days numbered and he knows when you will die, can you die before your time? It just couldn't be Billy's time.

People started showing up. Billy's teammates were making their way in to see him. There were several guys standing around his bed. I felt like I had to keep conversation going. I didn't like the silence. It was too much like a funeral, and I wasn't ready for that.

My mother and sister made their way closer to Billy. My short mother went around, greeting these giant, three hundred-pound football players. She introduced herself as Billy's Grammy. As she made her way to her firstborn grandchild lying in the bed, she rubbed his head and his cross tattoo on his left arm and asked everybody to join hands for a prayer.

The scene was surreal as Billy's family, some teammates, Pastor Guy, and anybody else standing nearby all held hands and prayed. We asked God for Billy back. We asked God to bless Billy with time in this world. We asked God to bless us with more time with Billy. We asked for a miracle.

2: Mercy Hospital

The praying started out quietly and peacefully with humility in our voices, but something changed. Something spiritually intense happened during that humbling prayer. My mother's language began to change. She was speaking an angelic language that was both powerful and real. I didn't expect it, and it sounded like a foreign language from a foreign land. It startled me at first. In that moment, my five-foot mother was the giant in the room. God was communicating through her. I felt a powerful sense of peace surround me. I felt the power of God cover us and the Holy Spirit whisper, "Billy's okay." Not okay in the sense that he would get up and walk out of the room, but okay in the sense that he had already gotten up and left the room, that he was safe, and he was home.

Even though the day would prove to be very hectic, stressful, and torturous in many ways, I was going through a transformation. My spiritual focus and understanding were partially blocked by an earthly wall. My lenses were being replaced with new, better lenses. My vision eternally changed, and I was able to see a little more from God's perspective. The two parallel worlds merged and became one. Part of me left this world with Billy. Part of me will always be with Billy, yet part of Billy will always be here next to me in this world as long as I live.

The grip we have on this life became so apparent and so real to me that day in the hospital. So many people tried to reach out and help. But there was an overwhelming feeling of helplessness. One person came up to me while I was standing in the hall. She told me about a surgeon at Georgetown Hospital who was one of the best. I could call him and ask for a second opinion on Billy's prognosis. On the surface, it sounded like a great idea, and I really appreciated her concern, but I didn't have it in me to call for a second opinion. Why take a chance with a surgeon from another hospital in another state, possibly advising us to hang on? We were hanging on with all we had left anyway. Two more doctors had to look at Billy before he was officially pronounced dead. He was brain-dead, and we were going to hang on to every ounce of hope until we finally heard from that last doctor and were forced to let go. It would prove to be a long, draining day, and I couldn't take the chance of false hope. I had to let go and accept the truth before me.

And it was a slow torture.

After watching my healthy, nineteen-year-old son leave in a flash, the fact of my own mortality grew nearer, and this same reality sunk in more deeply with each breath I took. It was as if God Himself told me that I had a fatal disease and that my body was dying. My death was imminent, and I knew that each breath truly could be my last. Each breath truly brings me closer to my last.

Through this shock and pain, I knew there had to be more. I always did, but now it was different. My hand was called. *What do I really believe? The story can't end this way. Billy's story can't be over like this; it has to continue. He has to go on.*

At this point, more and more people arrived from the team and from Maryland. The coaches came back to say good-bye. Many were speechless and teary-eyed.

2: Mercy Hospital

Billy's teammates formed a line that stretched into the hallway to say their final good-byes. Teammates like Larry Fitzgerald, who lost his mother just two months earlier to breast cancer, leaned over Billy and kissed his forehead. I was truly humbled by the expressions of love. It was overwhelming, and I found myself speechless for most of that dreadful day.

The family Billy stayed with during his summer workouts the year prior was having a day in the hospital as well. Quarterback Luke Getsy's sister gave birth that same day a couple floors up. Luke would pop up two floors to see his newborn nephew entering the world and drop down two floors to watch his former roommate and friend leave it.

There was a moment when it was just Nick and I in the area with Billy. With the curtain partially pulled back, Nick was sitting next to the bed, quiet and calm for the moment, and I was standing, facing away from the bed with my arms crossed, trying to stay strong for my family while engrossed by the enormity of the day.

A short, stocky priest came around the corner and introduced himself as Father Henry Krawczyk. I knew exactly who he was. He seemed a little guarded as he extended his hand and asked about Billy's prognosis. I said, "He's gone."

Krawczyk asked if he could give last rites. I paused. I really didn't know how to react. I was drained and too numb to feel anger. I slowly turned and waved the priest on, without saying a word. I didn't know what he was going through, and I didn't know the whole story, but this was my way of allowing the priest a chance to say good-bye.

I turned and watched Krawczyk standing to the right side of my brain-dead son, his head down, quietly giving Billy last rites; the image began to trouble me. This was the parish priest of St. Anne's Catholic Church in Homestead, the church in which Billy fell to his death just eight hours earlier. *Should he be here? Does this guy get it? Does he understand what he's doing?* It was disturbing for me to watch. Even with what little I knew about the circumstances that led up to Billy falling in this guy's church, under his watch, I knew something was terribly wrong with this picture.

I felt he was there more out of obligation. It was almost as if he were doing his duty or following orders. I didn't ask any questions because the truth would eventually come out anyway, and this was neither the time nor the place. No, I didn't feel comfortable with Krawczyk giving Billy last rites. My gut was telling me something wasn't right about it at all, but I gave him that opportunity, I gave him a chance, knowing that the motive of his heart was being measured by God Himself and that only God knows a man's true motive.

Krawczyk finished his prayer and walked out without saying another word. I knew it wouldn't be the last time I would see him.

The situation was way beyond my control, but my reaction to the situation at this point was what mattered. It was all I had left. It was too late for Billy. Unless God was going to bless us with a miracle and bring him back,

2: Mercy Hospital

Billy had left us, and now we had to figure out where to go from here.

I was very aware of the unseen audience for most of the day, watching my every move, listening to my every word. I understood that there was significance to my actions and reactions. I was also aware of my surroundings in the hospital. I noticed two faces in particular. A man and a woman seemed to pay particularly close attention to us. They were dressed professionally and did not appear to be part of the medical staff. They seemed to pop up throughout the morning at different times. I couldn't figure out who they represented, but it seemed they had a keen interest in Billy's condition, and I knew it was just a matter of time before the inevitable introduction.

The day wore on. This was not how I pictured it. The roles were reversed. It was very unnatural. I'm the one who should be dead. My sons were supposed to be grieving over their poor, dead father. I should be the one passing the torch down to them.

I spent most of that day in the hospital trying to be the strong one, trying to figure out the meaning of it all. It had to mean something much bigger than I could ever comprehend because I simply couldn't comprehend the way it happened.

One thing was very apparent to me that day in the hospital. Billy had many people who loved him dearly. There were parents and teammates from Maryland in the hospital that day. We had teammates and coaches from Pittsburgh. Relatives from as far away as Long Island, New York to Harrisonburg, Virginia, all came pouring into the hospital. Those who couldn't make it were calling and praying. Back home at Urbana High School, more than three hundred people held hands and stood in a circle around the football field and prayed. The same field people had circled to watch Billy play football was surrounded for a different reason. There were perhaps thousands of people praying for us that day. I could feel their prayers during this time of despair. I was aware of the people praying for us that day in the hospital. I could feel it. I could sense it. I lived it.

For a guy who was voted quietest of his senior class in high school and, by many accounts, still very private and independent, I was naturally uncomfortable with the attention my family and I were receiving. I believed I was self-reliant, and I thought I wanted to be left alone to grieve and take care of everything myself. I really didn't think I wanted or, dare I say, needed the help. But it wasn't about me. I had to accept the love and support people were offering. I had to step back and let people get involved. It was Billy who was lying in that bed, not me. But it was Billy's family that was still here, trying to survive.

The truth is, I'm sure my family and I needed help. We needed every bit of it. There is no doubt it would have been much harder without the love and support of the many people around us. These people loved Billy, but they were also there to love and support us. God used people as instruments of grace in so many ways, and I could really see that in the hospital and during the hard days that followed.

2: Mercy Hospital

Finally, the introduction was about to occur. She came up to me and introduced herself. I knew it was coming. I sensed whom she represented before the introduction.

Organ donation.

I could tell by the way they were watching us. It was an eerie feeling, really. They were like vultures circling the body, waiting for the all-clear signal before they swooped down.

They didn't have the all-clear signal yet. The third surgeon hadn't tested Billy, and there was still hope. It didn't matter. The introduction was brief. They expressed their condolences and explained who they were. I recognized the difficulty of their jobs and respected the responsibility they had. It was a job I don't believe I could have handled, yet a job that was extremely important and deserved my utmost respect. Referring to them as vultures was unfair and untrue. It was just the way I felt at the moment, but these people were professionals trying to do their job—a very difficult job, indeed.

Like many of us, Billy had checked the organ donor box on his driver's license application, never believing it would actually be needed, but, at the same time, acknowledging that if fate would have it and he would die, he would want to help someone in need. I was brief with the donor representatives. I knew what was coming; I just wasn't ready to accept it without a little fight. That's all I had left—a little fight.

It was getting late, and we were still gathered in the hall outside of the ICU, praying and hoping for a miracle. It was around 11:30 p.m. when the third surgeon poked his head through the swinging doors and announced in a rather loud voice, "Still no sign of brain activity; sorry." And the surgeon was gone.

So was our hope for a miracle. The hallway grew extremely silent as people froze in disbelief. It was as if we needed a nudge to move on. Within a few minutes, the organ donor people approached me to inform me that Billy had signed the donor card and was going to be an organ donor with or without our permission. They asked if we could sit down to finalize the paperwork. My heart told me that if Billy signed the card, he wanted this. So with my head still spinning from the announcement by the third surgeon, I quietly agreed to sign the paperwork.

I'm sure the wheels were turning behind the scenes. The donor recipients were most likely alerted and perhaps prepped. Time was obviously of the essence. At that point, I had to look through my own pain and recognize the process before me.

My wife, Kim, a few family members, and I met the two people from organ donation in a small conference room. Everything moved in slow motion, much like the day began with the early morning knock on the door.

I had to concentrate really hard to take in the whole organ donation procedure. They were going to remove my son's beating heart, ice it down, transport it to another hospital, and use it to replace a defective heart in another body. We were discussing his eyes and skin and how he would appear in an open casket. It was as if we were discussing a used machine and what parts would be available. Through it all, I knew it was the right thing to do.

2: Mercy Hospital

It was what Billy wanted, and more importantly, I believe it is what God wanted as well.

As I sat there, discussing my son's organs with the organ donor people, it really hit me what organ donation is truly all about. It's the ultimate gift of unselfish love. It is a powerful way to share your gift from God—the incredible gift of creation by the hand of our Creator. I was positive Billy would agree.

After we signed the paperwork and said good-bye to the many people in the hallway, we each quietly, and in our own way, said good-bye to Billy.

I sat next to the bed as the nurse began to scan Billy's young, strong, body with a handheld device. I was totally exhausted and numb from head to toe. I was looking at a living body of a young and healthy kid, but void of a living person. I was sitting next to a young body of good organs and beating heart, but no life.

It was very strange; I had no tears, and I hadn't cried once the entire day. I never had a moment where it was just Billy and me—not even at this point. I'm sure the nurse had a sense of urgency to prep Billy's body for the organ removal procedure, and perhaps I should have demanded a moment of privacy. But I didn't. I don't know what I would have done with it. God was going to read my heart whether the curtain was pulled or not, and my heart knew Billy was gone. There was no connection with the body in front of me.

It wasn't Billy anymore.

I quietly said goodbye and left the room with my head down, still hoping my alarm clock would go off, that I would wake up and discover it was all a dream. But the nightmare was real.

3: The Day After

> Now I want you to know, brothers, that what has happened to me has really served to advance the gospel.
>
> Philippians 1:12

It was sneaking up on midnight when we left the hospital. The University of Pittsburgh had booked rooms for our family and friends at the Holiday Inn on campus. I was drained emotionally and physically, but my body wouldn't shut down and sleep.

I needed the rest badly. The day's nightmarish events kept replaying in my mind. I finally crawled out of the bed and staggered to the bathroom around 2:30 a.m. This was a time I would find myself wide-awake often in the future, as if I were nudged by the Grim Reaper to remind me, almost taunt me, "Psst... It's 2:30 a.m. Do you know where your children are?" It was a consistent reminder that I was not in control.

3: The Day After

I peered into the bathroom mirror as if I were looking at a complete stranger. What I saw looking back was a broken, defeated, and tired man. His eyes were bloodshot and sad. His face was pale and filled with grief. I had never seen this face; this was someone different. I would soon discover who that man was. I would soon discover myself.

The questions were still there, but the answers, I simply wasn't privy to. These questions began to change. They were going in a direction that I just couldn't accept. Could this tragedy be from the hand of God? Was this in some way an answer to a prayer? Was this in some powerful way God's plan of using this tragedy for His purpose? I was reaching and desperate for answers.

The next day after Billy's death, the first call at the hotel I received was from my father. Dad and I typically spoke a few times a year—usually at Christmas, my birthday, and Father's Day, which also fell around his birthday. I don't recall how our conversation went that Father's Day. It was typically about how the kids were doing in sports. Billy's football accolades brought us closer over the years. It started with his first varsity game as a sophomore in which he received headline attention in the *Washington Post* for his game against Largo High, a strong Washington DC area team. I called dad the next day and told him to get a copy of the *Post*, because Billy was in the headlines. After that day, I would send him newspaper clippings from our local paper and video of some of the games almost weekly during Billy's three football seasons at Urbana. I also sent him recruiting articles during the off-season.

This short phone conversation we shared that morning was unlike any we had had before. The subject couldn't be avoided. The conversation would be about death, and eventually, the conversation would lead to God.

My dad described how he fell to his knees in his workshop, crying out to God after hearing about his grandson's death, how he had never cried like that in his life.

At this point, I hadn't cried yet, and I wasn't sure why, but this was an opportunity to discuss God with my father for the first time, and I knew he was ready to talk.

I believed my father to be an atheist for most of his life. As a child, I have memories of my father debating religion with my mother, saying things like, "We're like ants! Splat! We're gone!" Then he would laugh as if any other idea would be silly.

My dad had experienced grief before. He had lost his parents, a brother, and a few sisters over the years. He had just buried a severely handicapped stepson a few years back. My parents knew the pain of losing a child. Their first-born child was stillborn, and now, over forty years later, they were experiencing the tragic loss of their eldest grandchild.

My father didn't say it, at least not to me. Perhaps, like many men, he didn't know how. But he loved his family and was extremely proud of all of his grandchildren. The proud grandfather had many articles and newspaper clippings of his grandchildren on the walls of his small

3: The Day After

garage workshop. That workshop was his personal little shrine, and it clearly displayed his love for his family.

The powerful conversation with my dad was rejuvenating, and it gave me a reason, just for the moment, to believe Billy's death perhaps wasn't in vain. To a father who just lost his son, I believe this was the most important thing that could have come out of this heart wrenching loss. God was using this dark moment to tug heartstrings. I believe, in many ways, Billy's death kicked a door down for my dad. A doorway that was blocked by darkness was smashed down by a powerful light.

After I said goodbye and hung up, I turned to my wife, Kim, and started talking about the events leading up to Billy's death. For the first time, I felt a fire start to ignite in my soul. My shock gave way to anger, and the more I talked, the louder and the more furious I became. My sons, Michael and Nicholas, were listening. I could see them out of the corner of my eye, but neither one said a word as they let their father pour out his rage.

As I ranted, Kim stopped me mid-sentence. "Bill," she said quietly, but just loud enough to get my attention.

"What?" I shouted back, expecting her to tell me to calm down.

"Billy has your Father's Day gift waiting for you in his room."

I froze. I was speechless and couldn't move. It was as if God smacked me back into reality. Kim had my full attention. She said it in such a way that in one brief moment, I felt like Billy was still alive. My heart skipped a beat as I slowly turned to look her in the eyes. I wanted her to repeat it, but I couldn't breathe, let alone speak.

And then she said, "He saved every penny from his small stipend check he received from the football team for food and living expenses. It wasn't easy to do with no time to work in between summer school and football workouts. He sacrificed to save, and he shopped around for a while." I was completely caught off guard. This was not the conversation I was expecting. Kim continued, "Billy bought you new golf irons for Father's Day. It took him months to save. He was very excited and was going to surprise you this weekend."

That's when it hit me like a ton of bricks. It was that moment, that exact moment, that I felt the brunt of the blow. The full impact of Billy's death hit me like a tidal wave. I felt like he was alive while Kim was talking about the Father's Day gift, but when she stopped talking, it was as if my Father's Day gift from Billy was some cruel joke.

My rage melted into devastation, and the tears came out for the first time. It started out quietly and slowly as I felt the grief soak into my soul like a heavy cloud, but it quickly changed to loud, uncontrollable wailing as the grief overwhelmed my being and poured out like a powerful thunderstorm.

I got up from the desk chair and sat on the bed next to my wife. I leaned into her and let it out. I wanted to stop, but I couldn't. It felt unnatural for me. There was nothing natural about it. I was mourning the death of my son. Is there anything more unnatural than that? The harder

3: The Day After

I tried to stop, the more intense the pain became. It was something that had to happen, and I had to let go. The grief had to be released and this was the only way.

When the weeping finally subsided, I felt a tremendous release. There was an acceptance that set in. I was confronted again with that question. The words "I will go to him, but he will not return to me" are the words of David in 2 Samuel 12:23. After grieving over his dying infant child, David's attitude quickly changed from grief to acceptance. These words from David could be powerful words of hope. But did I believe these words to be true?

We met family and friends down in the lobby of the hotel. My brother, Buddy, and his wife, Marcy, drove up from their vacation in Ocean City, Maryland. Buddy gave me a hug and then turned away in tears. It was awkward, as my brother and I have a very laidback, easygoing relationship. There's usually a lot of fun stabbing and inside jokes between us, inside jokes that can only come from a brother. It has always been easy for us to laugh at each other, and neither one takes the other too seriously. But this was serious, awkward territory for us. This kind of tragedy was new to us. I really didn't know what to say to my younger brother other than, "We will survive this; we will get through it."

I grabbed a copy of the *Pittsburgh Post-Gazette* that morning, and on the right side of the front page, the headline read, "Pitt football player hurt badly by fall inside church." Ironically, on the left side, the sidebar read, "Bishops doing little on abuse, group charges." In many ways, as an evangelical Christian, I was naïve to the scandal within the Catholic Church, and I had no idea how deep the problem really was. I was unaware of the magnitude of their abuse scandal and other problems. Suddenly, my family was tied to the Catholic Church in a way I could have never imagined. I was about to find out that the abuse scandal was about more than the sex abuse; it was about the abuse of trust, and we trusted our son would be safe in a Catholic church. He wasn't. We were all drained and ready to go home, but after checking out of the hotel, family and friends gathered in the lobby, and some of us were going by the church to get Billy's things. It was a short drive to St. Anne's in Homestead, and as we were driving, I struggled to reflect on what led my son to that little Catholic Church outside of Pittsburgh.

As we were driving into Homestead, an old steel mill town, the neighborhood seemed quiet. It was a hilly community with sidewalks and chain-link fences. As we pulled up to the church, there was a large gathering of news reporters in front. The church parking lot had a huge metal fence surrounding it. It had an eerie look, almost like a jail.

We parked outside of the closed gate and met Billy's roommate David Abdul, who was the starting kicker on the team and went by the nickname Kicker. There were dozens of Billy's family and friends from Maryland there to see the church. Some were hanging around outside and some had made their way into the church sanctuary.

We got out of the car, and I noticed a massive white Great Dane staring me down from behind the short fence

3: The Day After

across the street from the church. He had a black face and cold eyes. It felt like the devil himself was eyeballing me. Billy mentioned this dog on several of our phone conversations, and it diverted my attention just for a moment. The dog barked, and it was deep and loud. It seemed thicker and bigger than your average Great Dane, and I suspected it was a mix of some kind. For a moment, it was as if Billy was there; I could almost hear him describing the big dog across the street.

Kicker asked if we wanted to get Billy's stuff from his room. Kim and I paused and made eye contact. We had no choice but to enter the church. I took a deep breath and nodded. Kicker led us into the old church. There was no sign of a priest or anybody else from the church in the area.

We walked up a long walkway and into a side door adjacent to the church sanctuary. We then turned left, away from the sanctuary, and down a hallway that resembled an old college dorm. There were small rooms on both sides all the way down the narrow, dark hallway. Most of the windows were bare except for dingy blinds and shreds of plastic. There were wires hanging and dead plants in the windows. My despair grew deeper as we walked closer to Billy's room.

We finally reached it. All of his belongings were boxed and pushed out to the hallway. My heart dropped at the sight. *This was it?* There was a fifty-dollar rent check sitting on top. His stuff was packed and cleaned out, and this was all we had left of our son. This was all that was left of our son.

BLOOD on a Pew

I stepped into his room. The room was narrow with a window over his bed. He had enough space for a bed and a dresser. My Father's Day gift, brand new golf irons, still in the box, leaned against the wall. Everything he owned was thrown in one box, and the box was shoved out into the hallway as if there was a sense of urgency to move him out of there. I felt sick to my stomach and had to step out.

As I stepped back out to the hallway, I noticed a little brown book sitting on top of Billy's box of stuff, and it instantly grabbed my attention. It was *The Screwtape Letters* by C.S. Lewis, dog-eared on chapter eight. I had never heard of C. S. Lewis and didn't know anything about the book, but I would later become a big fan of C.S. Lewis and read *The Screwtape Letters*.

I found a second book among Billy's belongings, and it caught my attention as well. It was thick with a brown cover and white laces down the back of the binder. It looked like a football. It was a brand new Holy Bible from my mother, Billy's grandmother.

I opened the cover and read, "Memorial Day, Monday May 26th 2003, after you were burned out of your Pittsburgh house and miraculously spared. I love you Billy. You are our Golden Boy. Love, Grammy."

After gathering Billy's belongings from the hallway of the convent and loading them into his gold 2002 Toyota Tacoma truck, Kim went back into the sanctuary. It must have been several minutes before I followed, and when I walked in, I glanced up at the ceiling where the new tile was in place. I couldn't believe how high the ceiling

3: The Day After

was. It was every bit of thirty feet. I wasn't ready to think about it. But there was no avoiding it. The new tile stood out, and it was the tile through which Billy had fallen. There were several people scattered around the cold, dark sanctuary, most of whom I didn't recognize.

Wailing in front of the church caught my attention immediately. I slowly walked towards the front of the sanctuary and towards the sound. I could hear loud sobbing echoing from the front lobby, a painful weeping sound that only a grieving mother could make.

I came around the corner, and everything went into slow motion. Billy's mother was on her knees, leaning over a broken pew, with a piece of the pew in her hand. She was sobbing. "My baby! My baby!"

I couldn't comfort her, as I had no comfort to give. She continued to sob as I watched, amazed at the insensitivity of leaving the broken pew in front of the lobby, almost as if it were on display. The ceiling was patched and the pew was replaced. Billy's room was cleaned out and the door that led to the roof was locked. Yet, somehow they forgot to hide the broken pew? There seemed to be no compassion for the victim's family, no respect for the deceased. Thousands of innocent young souls have been abused over the centuries by this unseen evil that has deeply infiltrated the Catholic Church, and now there was blood on a pew... my son's blood.

As I walked over to the spot where Billy fell, I looked up at the ceiling, and I had a vision of Billy's last moment on this earth. Billy's head came through the thin ceiling tile about thirty feet above, gaining speed with each inch, falling in the dark, cold sanctuary, past the large, stained-glass window depicting four saints, and before he realized what was happening, bam! He was gone. He crashed into the hard, wooden pew, headfirst, and rolled over onto the cold, hard concrete floor. I could see the blood dripping; I could envision every gory detail.

    I walked around the sanctuary and took in the enormity of the scene. I was fully aware of a young woman in the pew watching my every move, but I also felt the same invisible eyes that followed me through Mercy Hospital. At this point, my brother, Buddy, came over to me and asked if I wanted to go upstairs and see the crawlspace. My heart jumped. I really hadn't thought about that, and I had accepted the fact it was probably covered-up like his room and the ceiling and the pew. I was sure the door had to be locked now.

    Buddy noticed a shadow lurking behind a door off the rectory in front of the church. He went up to the door, and in a very direct tone, demanded the person unlock the door that led to the crawlspace. After pounding on the glass of the door until it sounded like it was going to shatter, Krawczyk slowly opened the door and peaked out. Buddy said, "My brother wants to see where his son fell to his death and somebody needs to unlock the door now!" Krawczyk called a maintenance person who unlocked the door.

    I took a deep breath as I prepared to track Billy's last steps. I went out of the sanctuary and through a door on the right. This took me through a small prayer room with more pews lined up about two deep. It looked like a mini

3: The Day After

sanctuary with kneelers and some statues and candles. I turned right and walked to the back and through another doorway before turning right again and walking up a narrow, steep set of concrete steps to the next level above the rectory. I turned left into a small utility room with a window straight back, and as I walked towards a window, there it was. A small, rickety ladder led to the crawlspace over the sanctuary. I slowly turned right, bracing myself for the sight. I couldn't believe how deep it was. Even with the temporary lights hanging from the left side of the ceiling every thirty feet or so, it was an eerie and dangerous sight. Two thick, heavy planks, which looked to be sixteen inches each, ran together down the middle as far as the eye could see. There was a bell tower on the other side, which led to the front of the church. I couldn't see the other side. There was insulation on both sides, and it came up flush to the planks, so I couldn't see what was below. The roof was slanted down from left to right, and it looked like enough space to stand—especially if you were just five feet, seven inches tall. But I noticed a couple huge metal roof beams hanging down pretty low. If Billy had tried to stand and walk back, his head would have bumped the beam, causing him to lose his balance.

Seeing the crawlspace helped give me closure. I didn't have to imagine what it was like. I was looking right at it. We went to the back of the utility room, through the open window, and out onto the flat gravel roof. I could see down into the valley, and I'm sure it was quite the scene at night with all the lights. I was ready to get out of there and head back home.

BLOOD on a Pew

As we climbed back through the window and walked by the crawlspace, the short ladder caught my attention again. I paused. *What was it that drew Billy into that creepy, dark crawlspace?* If Billy was miraculously spared from the fire, why wasn't he saved from this crawlspace?

As we started to load the car for the long trip back to Maryland, my grieving and exhausted wife said, "Out of all of the places Billy could have been that night, I trusted that my son would be safe in a church."

4: The Fall

> I tell you the truth, unless a kernel of wheat falls to the ground and dies, it remains only a single seed. But if it dies, it produces many seeds.
>
> John 12:24

My son Billy had this running joke with his team captain and fellow Pitt wide receiver, Yogi Roth. Yogi would ask Billy every day after practice if he was having fun, and Billy's reply was always, "No, football is not fun for me anymore."

As a freshman at the University of Pittsburgh, Billy had a challenging start to college football. I'm sure, in some ways, it wasn't what he expected. But on the morning of June 17, 2003, Billy's response was different. "You know what? I had fun today. I really did. I actually had a great time playing football."

Yogi noticed a difference right away. He could tell there was a bounce in Billy's step. Yogi sent a message to the defensive backs: "Billy Gaines is back, and he's bringing his A game. You better be ready!"

That was before Billy got back to his locker and realized his wallet was missing. It seemed to be his fate that summer. He was out of sorts since his townhouse near campus caught fire a few weeks earlier and he was forced to move into an old, closed-down Catholic Church convent off campus until he found other living arrangements.

That was my son's home for a couple of weeks and he never felt settled. Pittsburgh never really became home.

As Billy was preparing for his sophomore year, his summer living arrangements were unusual. He and roommate David Abdul," had been living in the shuttered convent for about three weeks, and they were still trying to get used to the idea.

My son was living in a convent adjacent to a church for the summer. It sounded safe to a father over two hundred miles away in Maryland. It turned out to be the most dangerous place he could have stayed that summer.

Billy's path to St. Anne's Catholic Church began in late June 2002, right after he graduated from Urbana High School in Ijamsville, Maryland. Billy was graciously invited to stay with fellow incoming freshman quarterback and Pittsburgh local Luke Getsy and his family for the summer.

Billy met Luke in June of 2001 at the Pittsburgh summer football camp, where Luke and Billy both were offered scholarships to play football for the Pitt Panthers.

The Getsy's were very generous to have opened their home for the summer, and we all appreciated their gen-

4: The Fall

erosity, but Billy was a homebody for the most part, and he was going away for the first time.

It didn't take long for Billy to get to know Luke and the Getsy family, but he definitely believed he would have trained harder back home in Maryland during those hot summer months. He was a gym rat, and he had plenty of open fields where he could train back home in Maryland. But it was important to participate in the summer voluntary workouts with the team if he wanted a shot at playing as a true freshman. Luke was a member of St. Anne's in Homestead where he had a summer job doing landscaping around the graveyard and church grounds. The resident priest offered Billy a job with Luke that summer, and that's where he met Reverend Henry Krawczyk, known as "Hank" to the guys. Hank was the pastor and sole priest for St. Maximilian Parish. The parish was a group of multiple churches in the Pittsburgh area over which the Reverend Henry Krawczyk presided.

It was just a few weeks prior, in May of 2003, when Billy found an old row house on Zulema Street in Oakland and moved in with six other teammates, all still teenagers starting their sophomore year. The place seemed perfect for the summer—cheap rent and very convenient, right on the University of Pittsburgh's campus.

Just days after moving in, Billy awoke from a nap and went downstairs. He could smell a strange odor, but couldn't figure out where it was coming from. That odor turned out to be something electrical, and it ignited a fire upstairs. The fire started in an electrical outlet next to Billy's bed, the same bed he was napping in just minutes before. The bed went up in flames, and within minutes, the fire spread, destroying all of his belongings. Fortunately, no one was hurt in the fire.

The university arranged for the guys to stay at the nearby Holiday Inn in Oakland until they found another place to stay. Most places were rented for the summer, so their choices were limited. The university couldn't pay the high Holiday Inn rates for long, so the guys had to find a place fast.

All five guys accepted an invitation from the "cool priest" of St. Anne's to temporarily move into the previously closed convent in Homestead, Pennsylvania. The convent closed in 1988 after allowing immigrants to stay there until they found housing in their new country, and it was now being used as a temporary college dorm.

Just a few days after moving to the convent, four of the guys found a place and offered Billy a place on the couch, but they didn't have room for Kicker. Billy didn't want to leave his friend and teammate alone in the convent, so he declined the offer. Instead, Billy decided to look for a place with Kicker, and they both decided to stay in the convent and travel home for the weekends until they found another place.

The last time I saw Billy alive was Memorial Day, 2003. It was late evening, and he was in the kitchen, getting himself ready for that three and a half hour drive back to Pittsburgh and a busy week of classes and workouts. I said, "I'm glad to see things are going well for you up there."

4: The Fall

He paused then said, "I guess it's going well." The pause bothered me. As a father, the pause was all I had as a warning that something wasn't quite right. I let it go, but I should have questioned him. Maybe the pause was the only opportunity I had to recognize that my son's living arrangements would be a problem.

By June 16, 2003, Billy and Kicker had been living in the convent a couple weeks, and Hank invited the guys out to dinner. They discussed plans for a Tuesday night cookout at the living quarters off the church rectory. The guys didn't think much of it, and the plans were left open.

After dinner, the guys went back to the convent living room to watch a little TV before bed. They had to get up early for football workouts in the morning and needed the rest. Hank popped in for a short visit. He poured the guys a glass or two of Captain Morgan. Feeling a little obligated and not wanting to offend their landlord, the guys sipped their drinks, knowing they had practice in the morning and would regret it. After a couple drinks, Hank started describing his plans for a hot tub on the roof above the rectory. He asked the guys if they wanted to go up on the roof and check it out. Who wouldn't want to see a hot tub on the roof of a church? So the guys followed the priest out to the hallway and headed towards the sanctuary. There was a locked door on the left side of the hall, and the priest pulled out his keys and unlocked the heavy door.

I'm sure the guys walked by this door dozens of times and had no clue where it led. Now they were walking through this mysterious locked door for the first time.

BLOOD on a Pew

As they entered the room, they realized it was a small prayer room with a couple of pews. They followed the priest to the back of the dark prayer room where they went up a steep, narrow concrete stairway. They then walked through a utility room to a back window. It was dark, and they had some natural light, but they could only see a few feet in front of them. They climbed through the unlocked window out onto the flat gravel roof.

They took in the view and listened to Hank describe where he was going to place the hot tub on the flat gravel roof. Then they went up a ladder that led to the slanted roof above and sat there awhile, enjoying the nice evening. As they were heading back to their rooms, Hank repeated the offer to have the guys over to his place for a cookout the next evening, and he extended the invitation to the other three guys who had moved out of the convent a couple of weeks prior. Billy and Kicker politely declined, but Hank mentioned he would be ready, just in case.

Billy passed the invitation to the Tuesday night cookout on to the other guys, but he and Kicker really wanted to go down to Oakland for the night. With no early morning practice, this was their night to kick back and relax, and they were ready to get out of the convent for a while, but the other guys decided the cookout offer was just too good to pass up.

At about 9:00 p.m., Kicker and Billy were ready to relax after a long day of practice and classes. Hank came over to the convent and poured the guys a couple drinks to kickoff the evening. It would be the first of many

4: The Fall

rum-and-cokes for the guys that evening. They grabbed their drinks and headed over to the Hank's living quarters. They walked down the dark, narrow convent hallway, passed the big, heavy door on their left, and headed through the sanctuary doorway at the end. They strolled through the empty, dark sanctuary and up to the rectory.

The laundry room had been turned into a bachelor pad with plush red carpet and an impressively stocked semicircular bar made out of what appeared to be high-quality wood. The bar had many bottles of liquor, and it was open for the teenagers.

An outdoor deck off the kitchen overlooked the Monongahela River. The grill was hot and ready for the burgers, and the other football players arrived just minutes later. Kicker was doing the grilling on the deck as the priest was serving drinks from the bar. After serving up a couple of drinks to each of the guys, Hank turned the bar over to his under-aged guests and invited them to serve him for a while. Drink after drink, these college sophomores took full advantage of an impressively stocked bar. Hank challenged them to a drinking contest. Claiming he could take them shot for shot, he pulled out his favorite drink—Jagermeister. Now, the football players added some competition to the night.

Nobody was driving home, as they had planned to sleep in the convent, so they thought that they could drink freely without worry of an accident.

Around 11:30 p.m., Billy was feeling a little blue about losing his wallet earlier in the day. He decided to call his girlfriend, Natalie, who was also a University of

Pittsburgh student but home in Maryland for the summer. "What else can happen? What else can go wrong?" Billy asked Natalie.

"Don't do anything stupid," she said, and then before she hung up, she repeated herself, "Don't do anything stupid."

At this point in the night, the rum-and-cokes were flowing. The guys found a deck of recipe cards and started mixing drinks from the cards. Someone turned the TV on in the rectory and found a porn channel. The channels flipped through the night but somehow ended up back on the porn channel.

It was getting late; it was around 2 a.m. and the guys started to explore other areas of the sanctuary. The rectory was right off the altar, and that's where Billy, Kicker, and fellow teammate John, the starting tackle, stumbled onto the altar microphone and decided to become rappers, making up rhymes and using inappropriate language. The church altar had become a karaoke stage.

One of the guys had enough and found the power to the microphone. He shut it off, but that didn't last long. Like the porn channel earlier, there always seemed to be a hand in the shadows to turn the switch back on and keep the show running. The guys were back up on the altar, loudly rapping their hearts away, like they were the stars of their own imaginary rap concert inside a church sanctuary packed with their own imaginary audience.

At this point, the rap show from the altar was getting old, and the guys needed a different adventure. The seed was planted the previous night, and the curiosity

4: The Fall

of the roof above began to gnaw at their minds. Kicker mentioned to John the plans for a hot tub on the roof. The three guys headed up to the rooftop to see the future home of this church roof hot tub.

The heavy door to the small prayer room was left unlocked from the previous night, and the guys walked up to the utility room where the glow from the moonlight was seeping through the back window. Billy led the way. The guys managed to make it through the back window and onto the rooftop above the rectory. The guys are oblivious to any potential danger of being on the roof, intoxicated at 2:30 in the morning, and nobody was around to stop them.

After just a few minutes of looking around and enjoying the view, Billy was out of sight. Without saying a word, he had slipped back through the window. Kicker looked around, and realizing Billy had left without saying a word, he followed through the window. As Kicker was climbing back into the utility room, he saw Billy climbing the rickety four-foot ladder that led into a dark crawlspace. Kicker climbed up to take a look. He shouted, "Where are you going?"

Billy was silent; he never answered the question, and he crawled in like he was on a mission.

At first, Kicker could see Billy and the thick planks as he crawled behind, but it didn't take long before he had to depend on feel and sound as he crawled into total blackness.

BLOOD on a Pew

All he heard was the scraping of knees on the wooden planks. It was pitch black, and he had to reach out to feel where Billy was in front of him.

They had crawled into the black abyss of the crawlspace without muttering a word to each other. But Kicker finally had enough and said, "We might as well turn around, since we don't know where we're going."

Billy didn't argue, and he said, "Okay."

Kicker turned and started to crawl back, but as soon as he turned, he heard it.

The awful, gut wrenching sound that could only mean one thing.

Kicker looked back and saw a light shining up through the ceiling and into the dark attic, but it was what he didn't see that caused his heart to jump into his throat. He had to know as he turned and crawled the few feet back to the light. He poked his head through the hole and looked down. There it was—he couldn't believe it.

Billy fell thirty feet through the insulation and ceiling tile, smashing his head into the hard, wooden pew below.

Kicker saw Billy sprawled out on the bloody concrete floor next to a broken pew. "Call an ambulance!" he yelled back to John, who was still standing at the ladder, waiting for his teammates to return.

Kicker crawled out much faster than he had crawled in. He ran down the steps and back into the sanctuary where he found Billy on the concrete floor.

He grabbed Billy's bloody head and attempted to revive him, but Billy was completely unresponsive.

4: The Fall

Kicker looked down and saw blood on his hand, on the pew, and all over the floor. He knew Billy was in very serious trouble.

One of the guys performed CPR until he got a faint heartbeat. Amazingly, Billy started breathing again.

The paramedics arrived quickly, loaded Billy into the ambulance, and sped off to Mercy Hospital in downtown Pittsburgh.

This was the end of a big part of my life and the beginning of a new chapter.

This is where the journey begins for a brokenhearted father seeking answers to some of life's most difficult questions.

Photo Gallery

Billy's first catch

Photo Gallery

Family Christmas 2001

After another home victory at Urbana

BLOOD on a Pew

The prom picture with five of his best friends and Urbana teammates. L-R Scott MacGregor, Rem Ross, Travis Sheets, Billy, Brad Anderson, and Pat Ferguson

Billy and his dad Bill

Photo Gallery

Billy and Natalie after the Super 45 All-Star game summer of 2002.

High school graduation party spring 2002

BLOOD on a Pew

Urbana kids travel to Pitt L-R Kyle Cissel, Jacob Fagan, Shawn Kerman, Jeremy Grove, TJ Kerman and Davey Poole in back.

Fan day at Pitt August 2002

Photo Gallery

Warming up at Heinz Field in Pittsburgh

5: Saying Goodbye to a Son

> So we fix our eyes not on what is seen, but on what is unseen. For what is seen is temporary, but what is unseen is eternal.
>
> 2 Corinthians 4:18

We drove home from Pittsburgh that Thursday evening, June 19, 2003, and pulled into the driveway. Several neighbors came out to meet us. We received hugs and tears as we got out of the car, and Kim pulled up in Billy's pickup truck with his stuff loaded in the back. Not knowing what to say or afraid to say the wrong thing, nobody said much. Our neighbors could have hidden in their homes, and I wouldn't have blamed them, but these people can still remember Billy as an eleven-year-old, riding his bike around the neighborhood with a football under his arm.

5: Saying Goodbye to a Son

We were emotionally drained and had no strength left to unload, so the neighbors helped unload the truck and the station wagon for us.

I appreciated the hugs, kind words, warm meals, and thoughtful cards and notes from the many people who genuinely cared and felt for us. I could see the hurt in people's eyes and hear it in their words. And with the people who didn't make contact, I understood completely. It can be difficult to contact somebody after such a tragic loss when you don't know what to say or do.

The day after we returned from Pittsburgh was a day of planning. I knew I wanted to have Billy's funeral within a few days. I felt my family needed it as well.

Pastor Guy and a few neighbors were assisting with the memorial service and came by the house to discuss the plans. We pulled out Billy's brand new Bible, the one painted brown with white laces down the back of the binder. Our pastor loved it and said he could use it during the service. We had planned who would speak, the speaking order, and how the high school auditorium would accommodate the many people expected in attendance. The plans were scheduled quickly. It would have been easier to plan if we had pushed it out to a week, but with tremendous support from neighbors and friends and the services offered by Mountain View Community Church, the viewing was scheduled for Saturday night, June 21, 2003. The memorial service was scheduled for the next day at one o'clock, just four days after Billy's death, at the Urbana High School auditorium, where Mountain View held their regular Sunday services.

BLOOD on a Pew

After the morning meeting to plan the funeral arrangements, I started my day at the funeral home picking a casket. A couple of neighbors were gracious enough to drive me over for support.

We sat down with the funeral director and planned the viewing details for Saturday night. Then, we had to go into a back room and choose a coffin. As we were walking around the small showroom of caskets, I had a nauseating feeling; it was as if we were looking for a piece of furniture.

Why am I here picking Billy's casket?

Though I knew it would be a temporary box to house his body, it was a reality check of the finality of it all, and it was killing me inside. After looking at several coffins, I started to feel nauseous and dizzy. I didn't like any of the coffins. I started to panic a little. *What if I can't find one?* We finally got to one of the last ones they had in inventory. It was blue and silver with the words, "I'm home," printed on the inside of the door with a flock of birds flying above the words. "This is the one!" I whispered as I turned away with tears in my eyes.

I had instant peace. It was as if Billy was giving his dad a message. The words were true, the box seemed right, and Billy was home. It was a powerful reminder that Billy's body was going in that box, but Billy was already home. I didn't need to be reminded again after that moment. Billy was home.

The plans were made, and I had very mixed feelings about the service and what it meant. I knew there was something I had to say, but how could I convey it?

5: Saying Goodbye to a Son

I wasn't comfortable with public speaking, and probably not very good at it, yet this was a moment when I had to speak. I had to use this tragedy to share the reason for the hope that I had.

I started scribbling my thoughts and practicing what I was going to say, changing it dozens of times. Nothing seemed adequate; nothing seemed to express what was in my heart, the way God wanted me to communicate.

I live by the motto, "Be brief, be blunt, and be gone." I struggled with how to communicate something so powerful, so real, in such a short time. *How do I find the words to describe the most powerful truth I could ever know? How do I describe the incomprehensible power of God's grace?* I didn't feel at all prepared for the enormous responsibility.

Then God whispered in my ear, "The tattoo."

I could describe Billy's tattoo and its significance. What it meant and why Billy chose this particular tattoo said it all. Barbed wire wrapped his left bicep with a cross sticking through it. How was I going to explain a tattoo with so much mystery, yet significance beyond our comprehension? And what did the tattoo truly mean to Billy?

Billy and a few of his friends went to the tattoo parlor right after high school graduation. I warned him to be careful. "This is going to be a permanent marking on your body and people change; you will change," I said as they headed out the door. I was pleasantly surprised by his choice; he got the one thing that never changes, that will never fade away, and that, after more than two thousand years, has never been forgotten.

BLOOD on a Pew

Billy had a cross burned into his left bicep. I thought about that as I rubbed his cross tattoo while he laid brain dead in that cold hospital bed. I was reminded of the unimaginable warmth and peace it brought me during an excruciating day in which I needed it the most. And now I was thinking about it again as I prepared my words for yet another agonizing day.

The viewing was Saturday night, and we saw people there that we hadn't seen in a very long time. It was a family reunion, a party with old friends, and a reality check of what awaits us all. We were having a casual conversation about old times, keeping the memory alive of the cold, dead body that lie in an open coffin maybe twenty feet away.

A black teenage kid came up to me and shook my hand. He looked me in the eye and introduced himself as a football player who had competed against Billy. He said, "Your son was a warrior." I smiled with a sense of pride as those five words probably described my son better than anything I had ever heard, and it was a great compliment coming from another football player who battled against Billy on the gridiron.

The next morning was the day of the memorial service.

A friend was kind enough to pay for a limo drive for my family to the funeral home where we would say our last goodbyes as a family and then head over to Urbana High School for the service.

When we arrived at the funeral home, the coffin was opened for us to see Billy one more time. We each wanted some private time with him.

5: Saying Goodbye to a Son

I waited for my turn, and when it came, I got down on one knee, put my hand on his chest, and prayed quietly. I asked God to take care of my son in heaven as a father takes care of his child. I asked God to give Billy a message, to tell Billy that I knew where he was. I asked God to tell Billy that I was going to share this powerful truth by proclaiming it from the rooftops and by telling this story to the world. I asked God to tell Billy that we loved him, that we knew he loved us, and that we would see him again.

After my short prayer, I experienced the same peace I had in the hospital, that whisper from God that said, "Billy's okay."

I was going to need it.

As I was walking outside, preparing to ride over to the memorial service, something strange happened. I walked by this full-sized blue van and a man called me over. I walked over and he asked if I knew the father of the kid who died in Pittsburgh. After I told him I was Billy's father, he introduced himself and the lady he was with and told me they worked with schools to help educate kids on the dangers of underage drinking. Then, he asked if he could get some footage of Billy in his casket as part of the video. I paused, but of course, I wanted to help get that message across, so I agreed.

I allowed two total strangers to come into the funeral home and videotape my dead son lying in his casket.

After the woman called me by the wrong name and the man was moving from one side of the casket to the other, zooming in and out and getting every possible angle, I realized this was too intrusive for me. I finally spoke up. He ignored me at first and continued to videotape. I felt my blood pressure go up, and I repeated my request. He finally heard the tone, felt the tension, and stopped recording. I walked the couple out.

My family and I climbed into the back of the limo for the short drive down Interstate 270. The limo was quiet as we tried to stay calm for what would be a long, emotional day. The parking lot at Urbana High was packed. The limo pulled up, and we walked slowly to the front door.

I walked into the empty lobby towards the auditorium doorway. I couldn't believe my eyes. Packed! Not an open seat in the room. They had to move overflow to classrooms with video. I started to scan the room and recognized many familiar faces. The Pittsburgh football team was sitting in the back, and friends, family, and many faces I didn't recognize were seated elbow to elbow. We were escorted to the front where most of our extended family was already seated.

Billy's picture was placed in front for everyone to see, and there was a song playing in the background. Kim surprised me by getting up, walking to Billy's picture, and joined my mother, who had her head down and arm raised. Kim and mom were arm and arm with their free hands raised to the sky as they bowed their heads in prayer and praise.

Billy's mother and grandmother praised God on one of the saddest days they may ever know. I didn't join them

5: Saying Goodbye to a Son

because the Spirit didn't nudge me to. It was powerful, yet gut-wrenching to witness.

Pastor Guy then began the service with a couple Bible verses. The first verse was Psalms 116:15: "Precious in the sight of the Lord is the death of His saints."

How was Billy a saint? He died a teenage college student getting drunk inside a Catholic church. By that time, other people knew Billy was drunk when he fell to his death. I'm sure more than a few eyebrows went up.

But the truth is, it wasn't about what other people thought. It wasn't about what other people said. Billy didn't need acceptance or forgiveness from other people. It wasn't other people who controlled his eternal destiny.

The second verse Pastor Guy read was 1 Thessalonians 4:13: "Brothers, we do not want you to be ignorant about those who fall asleep, or grieve like the rest of men, who have no hope."

Billy's high school coach, Dave Carruthers, started the service with a heartfelt eulogy. He spoke about Billy's work ethic and winning attitude. He talked about Billy's faith and drive and how he was striving for a Division I football scholarship. Then, the coach turned to us and humbly thanked us for allowing him to coach our son. Afterwards, he held up a football that was a little flat and said it represented the grieving people in the auditorium that day.

My heart definitely felt like that deflated football.

Person after person got up to the stage and was tossed the flat football. Pitt's head coach Walt Harris mentioned Billy's size—how it was never an issue with him and how special he was as an athlete and a person. He spoke about Billy's confidence as a football player. He also spoke about how emotional Billy got after receiving his first and only football scholarship offer from the University of Pittsburgh.

Coach Brookhart talked about how Billy touched his life in such a powerful way, and he told a story about how he went up to Billy after camp and said, "Billy, you're too short; you can't play at this level."

Billy snapped back, "You're wrong, coach!"

Many had words of inspiration, and it was comforting for a father to hear, but perhaps the most courageous person in the auditorium that day was Billy's girlfriend, Natalie Augustine. She got up on stage and tearfully read poems Billy wrote to her, and it was as if Billy were standing right next to her the whole time. I had no idea my son had that side. His poems were deep and spiritual, and I was blown away.

So many people spoke that day—coaches, friends, family, teammates—each with a story about how Billy touched their life, and the ball seemed to inflate a little after each person spoke. The hope was contagious and powerful. I was truly humbled by how many lives Billy touched in his short time here on earth.

The coach who recruited Billy to Pittsburgh perhaps made the most profound statement. Coach Shawn Simms, who had just accepted a job with the University of Colorado and had flown in for Billy's memorial service, said, "Billy doesn't want us to get up here and talk about him. Billy was ready, and like Jesus, Billy made the

5: Saying Goodbye to a Son

most of his short life. The Lord called him home, and he was ready."

What the coach said was powerful, courageous, and true. The coach became emotional to the point of tears and said, "Billy wants us to be ready when our day comes."

I know I lost that sense of security about my own mortality after Billy's death. I know my day is coming, and I do believe it can happen to me. The mindset of "That might happen to some people, but it won't happen to me" is gone.

It was near the end of the service, and now it was our turn to speak. The Gaines family slowly walked up to the stage.

As we passed my dad in the front row, I heard, "Go get 'em!" I just chuckled and turned to walk up the short steps. I felt unusually calm and relaxed, maybe too relaxed as the deflated football was tossed to me and I almost dropped it. *I'm sure Billy would have loved that.* I approached the podium holding the deflated football under my arm.

"Billy was an answered prayer." I said in a loud, direct tone as I scanned the audience. I was referring to the nine months I placed my hand on his pregnant mother's belly, praying feverishly for Billy. I had everybody's attention, and then I said, "I prayed Billy's football would lead others to God, and I thought that prayer was answered." When I made that statement, I was referring to the many prayers as a father praying for his son. I paused for a second. I wasn't sure I really got my point across, and I didn't really know how to make my point. This was not how I wanted God to use Billy. This wasn't my prayer. My prayer was that Billy would give God the glory after scoring a touchdown or making a big play or after a big game, not after his death. But how many of the people in the auditorium knew Billy from his football? Wasn't it football that made Billy Gaines popular?

I spoke about Billy's faith, and then I closed by saying, "The cross burned into his left bicep had special meaning, and Billy is waiting for us in heaven, and we can't let him down, and that's what gives us peace."

I tossed the flat ball to my sixteen-year-old son, Michael, and stood back. Michael became so emotional, he couldn't speak. He tried, but the words weren't coming. So Nick, fourteen at the time, took the flat ball and spoke about the enormous responsibility he felt to fill Billy's shoes on the football field. Nick was very composed as he shared stories of his brother.

Then, Michael courageously got back behind the podium and grabbed the football. He echoed Nick's sense of responsibility to carry the torch on the football field. I was proud of how both of my sons spoke from their hearts in front of a large crowd when it had to be extremely difficult to find the right words.

Both of Billy's younger brothers felt compelled to fill Billy's shoes on the football field, but for me, football lost so much of its luster and importance after Billy's death.

Kim was the last to speak, and she stood behind the podium and said, "How ironic was it that Billy fell and didn't get back up, and how happy did he make the devil that not only did he fall and not get back up, but he died

5: Saying Goodbye to a Son

in a church?" She then said, "I'm angry, but I haven't lost my faith. The devil won't get that. He can cheer all he wants."

Earlier in the service, when my mother had her opportunity to speak, she also had called out the enemy. "Satan thought he had victory, but he doesn't; just like on the cross, Christ has the ultimate victory."

My mother and wife really put a damper on Satan's victory party.

The memorial service at Urbana High School ended, and many people said some very nice things about Billy. We headed over to the gravesite for a short memorial service. The procession of hundreds of vehicles headed up Interstate 15 towards Frederick. Billy's casket was draped with an Urbana helmet on top of a number two jersey and a Pittsburgh helmet sitting atop a number twenty-nine jersey.

Pastor Guy closed the service with a prayer, and then he walked over and handed me Billy's bible.

At the end of the service, Kim called all of the Pittsburgh players over, and they gathered around in a big huddle, surrounding Billy's five-foot-two-inch mother as if she were the quarterback calling a play.

In a sense, she was calling a play. Kim began telling them that each could just as easily end up in a grave if they were not careful. She begged them not to put their parents through the agony and grief we were going through.

Coach Harris said, "That was an unbelievable wake-up call for our players. The players took this very hard. When you are young, you don't have to deal with death and issues of your own mortality. That's the great part of youth—they think they are going to live forever. These are highly conditioned, cream-of-the-crop athletes and have tremendous confidence in themselves. When one of their peers leaves them through death, it is a real eye-opener to them, and it really affects them."

The day at the gravesite ended with all of the players in the huddle putting their hands in, and on three, they all shouted.

"BG!"

6: Football-A Lesson in Life

> Physical exercise has some value, but spiritual exercise is much more important, for it promises a reward in both this life and the next.
>
> 1 Timothy 4:8

Though I tried to be there for my sons and catch every game and most practices, I wasn't the perfect father, and I had my moments. I'm a little hesitant to tell this story, but I think it's important to understand how sports can be a negative thing when we forget what matters. We can easily get caught up in the moment and lose our better judgment.

In one game, Michael's team was getting beat badly in this out-of-conference scrimmage game, and usually, I would take a deep breath and hope the kids learned a valuable lesson about life from the whipping. But this time was different. I recognized the coaches on the other team. I knew they could be extremely competitive. I couldn't help but be suspicious of the age and weight of some of their players. After all, they played in a different league and in a different county, and maybe they had different age and weight restrictions and were just older and bigger than our kids. But I was justifying my anger. I had no proof, and if they played in a different league, they could have legally had different age and weight restrictions.

Just as my competitive frustration peaked, a kid came up to the stands with a game jersey and passed me a message from Michael's football coach.

"They want to sneak Billy into the game," the kid said.

Now typically, I would have laughed at such a ridiculous suggestion—please believe me—but the timing wasn't good, as my common sense was blurred by suspected unfairness.

Billy had just finished his practice and was sitting in the stands watching his younger brother's scrimmage. He recognized the coaches from the other team as well and he had both played with and against these guys in the past. He had to have been getting a little restless watching the one-sided game, and when he heard his name mentioned, his head popped up like a curious puppy. We made eye contact, and I could tell he was ready and willing to get in the game.

The problem, of course, wasn't Billy's eagerness to play. The problem was me. Though it's true Billy was about the same size as most of the kids on the field, he was also two years older. But I couldn't stop myself. I consented, and before I could say another word, Billy had

6: Football-A Lesson in Life

on the game jersey and was on his way to the sidelines. I really didn't take it that seriously; it was a joke to me at first.

Billy stood on the sidelines. You could tell he was older just by his more mature build. It really looked obvious from where I sat, and I started to feel squeamish as I realized the stupidity behind the little ploy.

It was too late. He went into the game. The first play, he got the ball and trucked about six kids, but they eventually dragged him down to the turf. The parents from the other team immediately became suspicious and began grumbling and pointing.

"Where'd that kid come from?" I heard from five rows back. Billy would get another carry and drag another six kids down the field, but this time, he didn't stop until he scored. At this point, it wasn't funny anymore, and I wanted him to come out of the game. I could see the parents from the other team start to stand from their seats and point.

"No way! They would never sneak in an older kid!"

"What if somebody got hurt?" I heard from my back row seat, as we all sat in the same bleachers.

I don't think I was alone in feeling the heat as I watched Billy sneak out just as quietly as he had snuck in. Nobody noticed, as the focus was diverted to the coaches. I watched Billy remove the jersey, blend into the crowd, and stroll towards the concession stand. I slowly moved down the stands to avoid bringing any attention to myself, and I started to plan an exit strategy. The parents were definitely getting restless as I marched right through their furious protests.

Billy quietly slipped into the bathroom to change. I walked in as he came out of the stall in his shorts and t-shirt, holding his jersey and equipment by his side. He had this look on his face that said, *What did I just start?* One of the parents from the other team saw him come out. I think he probably knew, but decided to keep his mouth shut. I told Billy to walk with me out to the parking lot. One of the parents from our side walked with us, knowing a riot was imminent, as the chatter in the stands began to grow louder and more confrontational.

We walked out to our van in the dark parking lot, completely unnoticed by the angry mob. We waited for the rest of the family to make their way through.

Billy was very quiet during this entire episode. The referees actually called the scrimmage early because of the fuming parents. I got out of the van to investigate and walked about twenty feet from the back of the eight-foot chain-link fence where our coaches were gathered with the team. As they were trying to apologize to the kids for their boneheaded decision, they were being scolded by several angry parents from the other team. The enraged parents were yelling and pointing from the other side of the dark parking lot fence. The high chain-link fence acted as a cage, preventing an ugly riot. I was standing a few feet away from the heated parents, trying to decide if it was a good time to apologize. But if they turned on me, I didn't have a fence as a buffer, and I could find myself in a very bad situation. So I just quietly observed from the

6: Football–A Lesson in Life

shadows, completely unnoticed and feeling like the cause of all the commotion and anger before my eyes.

Eventually, the police arrived, and we all escaped without any physical harm. I know, as the father, I had some serious soul-searching to do. My competitive nature with my kids' sports clouded my better judgment. Sure, I never should have been put in that situation to begin with, but I was, and I failed to make the right decision.

There is no doubt God has wired us all to be competitive creatures.

There are the obvious problems of putting victory ahead of a child's self-esteem and the obsessive parent from the sidelines. I'm sure I struggled with both of those issues at times. I think most parents—if they're honest—have had moments they wish they could take back.

There was another area in which I could have done better. I believe that, as a young father raising three sons, I should have made one thing very clear.

God always comes first.

God should have taken priority over sports, and I think I failed to convey that message to my sons, because, quite honestly, God didn't always take priority in my life at that time.

I'm not saying we never should have missed one Sunday of church, but the sporting event itself, be it a game or practice, became more important than worshipping God. The sport took priority over everything, and that was wrong.

In spite of my inconsistent spiritual leadership, my kids all grew to know Christ. I give credit to the women in my family. It was my wife who nudged us to find a church, and it was my mother who planted the seed of faith, through her many conversations with her grandchildren about God.

It was the spring of 2001, prior to Billy's senior year in high school, youth league was way behind him. He was hearing from several college coaches, who had called him and expressed interest. About a dozen schools had invited Billy to their summer camp to work out in front of their coaching staff and visit their campus.

As an undersized receiver, we discussed how important the football camps were to showcase his ability, and he seemed to accept the challenge. Just like anything in life, confidence would be essential. Billy had to believe without a doubt that he could play at the highest level and compete with the best football players in the nation. He had that mindset in the spring of his junior year when he said to a reporter, "I know I'm going to have to go to camps and prove myself. They can't believe a guy my size can do the things I do. I feel like I'm the toughest man on the field, and I play with a passion. I may look small, but I play like a giant."

Some schools showed more interest than others, and based on the recruiting and location, Billy decided to camp at Pittsburgh, University of West Virginia, and the University of Virginia in five days. All are excellent schools, but it was at our first stop at Pitt where Billy felt he had the best opportunity.

On June 16, 2001, we arrived after a driving from Maryland, to check in at Sutherland Hall on the campus

6: Football–A Lesson in Life

of the University of Pittsburgh. As we were inching our way down the check-in line, several of the Pitt coaches recognized Billy in the crowd and made their way up to greet us. It was very encouraging to feel they were excited to see Billy at their camp. I was a little surprised they found him, nevermind recognized him, as he didn't typically stand out in a crowd of much taller athletes.

I spent the next day and a half watching football drills at their impressive football facilities. They shared their indoor and outdoor practice facilities with the Pittsburgh Steelers. The Steelers were in the same building and parked in the same parking lot. There was no question this was big time football.

It was the last day of football camp at Pitt. Billy was out of bed ahead of the sun (and all other campers) practicing his starts and cuts under the darkness of dawn. With the sun creeping up, one of the football coaches spotted him and recognized his passion.

Football was in his blood.

At the end of the camp, Billy was invited into Coach Harris's office with running backs, Coach Shawn Simms, and offensive coordinator JD Brookhart. Billy watched a short, powerful highlight video on the football program with inspirational music, loud crowds, and game footage of their 2000 season. Then, with visions of the Panthers scoring touchdowns and winning games still spinning in his head, he sat down with the coaches to discuss his future. It was here when Coach Harris offered Billy a full scholarship to play football at the University of Pittsburgh.

BLOOD on a Pew

As confident as Billy was in his abilities on the football field, this was a shocker, as the constant negativity about his height probably planted a seed of doubt. He prayed for it, worked for it, believed it would happen, but now it was here, and he became emotional to the point of tears. He was ready to commit right there on the spot. Coach Harris was taken aback by Billy's emotion.

"Most kids don't get emotional after a scholarship offer," the coach said.

The coach asked why he was so emotional. Billy said, "I thought I was going to have to walk-on to play Division I-A football." Players who don't get a scholarship "walk-on" to try out for the team with the hope of earning a scholarship later.

Coach Harris began to tear up as well. It was emotional for everybody in that office, and Billy made a promise to the teary eyed coach. He looked him in the eyes and said, "I won't let you down, coach."

I was still waiting at Sutherland Hall. The bus finally pulled up, but no Billy. Minutes later, he pulled up with Coach Simms. He got out of the car holding a big envelope.

He handed it to me with his little crooked grin and casually said, "Hey, dad, do you want to take a ride up to Heinz Field with Coach Simms?"

Not realizing his point, I checked my watch and said, "I guess, but we need to head down the road to West Virginia for their camp."

Then, with that same little grin, he said, "Maybe we should ride down and see the new stadium first, since I

6: Football–A Lesson in Life

may be playing in it next season. They just offered me a full scholarship."

My jaw dropped, and my heart jumped through my throat. I'll never forget that moment, as I had to fight my own tears.

As we rode over to Heinz Field with Coach Simms, I was still trying to comprehend what had just happened. I can remember sitting in the front seat talking about growing up watching the Steelers dynasty of the seventies as we drove through Pittsburgh. As we approached the new stadium, the same stadium the Panthers would share with the Steelers, it was a very exciting moment.

They were still building the stadium, and pre-season was only two months away. We took a tour through the completed locker rooms and down to the plush field. It was a sunny, clear day, and all I could see were rows and rows of shiny yellow seats and a perfect green turf.

This is big time football.

As we were walking back, Billy had a conversation with another receiver recruit he had met at the camp. A tall thin kid from Minnesota who joined us for the stadium tour, Larry Fitzgerald was being recruited by every top school in the nation. Larry was shocked when Billy told him this was his first scholarship offer.

During his playing career at Pitt, Larry won the Biletnikoff award for the top receiver in Division I-A football, he was nominated for the Heisman trophy, and he ended up the third overall pick in the NFL draft by the Arizona Cardinals. He is currently one of the top receivers in the NFL, setting records and he played in the Super Bowl with the Cardinals in 2009.

To Billy, as a freshman competing for playing time, Larry was just a fellow wide receiver who Billy described to me once as having the "best hands on the team." Billy practiced with and prepared with this high caliber wide receiver day-in and day-out during his brief college career. The bar was set high as Billy's benchmark for college receivers was not only the kid with the "best hands on the team," but the best receiver in the nation.

After Billy died the summer prior to their sophomore season, Larry Fitzgerald shared some of his feelings with a news reporter.

"So we were running every play, just me and him together, just being dog tired," Fitzgerald said. "I kind of recruited him to come here, too. When he and his father came to visit, I told him, 'This is the place you want to be,' so I feel partly responsible for him coming here.

"Sometimes you take for granted that God has given you size and speed," Fitzgerald said. "Then you see someone like Billy. People have been telling him he's too small or too this or too that. And he's out there fighting and scratching for everything. It gave you the incentive to do the same thing.

Larry Fitzgerald closed with these words. "The loss we had was tremendous. Billy was such a great person, and the way it happened, it was such a huge blow to us. It's still hard to speak about it."

He was right. Billy was told by most football recruiters that he was "too small" or "too this" or "too that" to

6: Football–A Lesson in Life

play college football, but he was never told he was "too slow," especially after the Nike camp held earlier at Penn State in the spring of 2001.

He had some success as a sophomore at this same camp and was labeled "underclassman to watch." Invited back as a junior, Billy had worked really hard to prepare for the Nike camp, and he felt confident that he would perform well.

Many times, we had discussed that it didn't matter to the recruiters how many touchdown receptions he had or how many games his team won. It came down to how fast his forty-yard dash times were. It was all about speed. Especially for a short wide receiver who was mistaken for a kicker when he walked into a room of football players.

The smaller you were, the faster you had to be to get a shot at playing college football. At Billy's size, he would have to be very fast.

Billy had just finished his two forty-yard dash times at the Nike camp when he walked up to me with his little crooked signature grin.

"Guess how fast my forty-yard dash time was, Dad?"

I paused for a second and said, "I would say maybe 4.49," really hopeful he was under 4.5, as the recruiters like to see 4.4 seconds or faster especially for the little guys.

"Nope, a little faster," he responded with a devious grin.

"Really? Okay, how about 4.39?" He took his thumb and pointed down to the ground as if to say, "Lower... much lower."

BLOOD on a Pew

At this point, I just start spitting out ridiculously fast forty times. "4.33, 4.29, 28, 25?" I stopped and just stared. "You have to be kidding me!" I said in disbelief.

"Try 4.22!" he said, and then he walked away with a swagger that I hadn't notice before.

My jaw dropped to the ground. Billy had just set the record for the fastest forty-yard dash time in Nike camp history at the time. At that point, I knew somebody, somewhere, somehow was going to take a shot on this little scrappy football player from Urbana. I started making highlight tapes and mailing them to every D-1 football program I could find an address for.

I believe even Billy was surprised by his Nike camp performance. He was unusually quiet and focused in the weeks leading up to the camp. He ate the right foods and worked hard at being in the best possible shape he could be for this once in a lifetime opportunity.

In the spring of 2001 Billy said this about the Nike camp to a recruiting website, "I felt my performance in the forty reflects how badly I want to be the best. My times were faster than I expected them to be, but I had some high expectations set for myself, and it feels good to reach them."

Here is another quote to a recruiting website that same summer going into his senior year of high school, "I definitely surprised myself; no one expects to come out of nowhere and be the fastest in the nation, but I was on a mission. With the adrenaline rushing, it just pumps you up."

6: Football-A Lesson in Life

But even with that blistering record-setting forty time at the Nike camp, Billy didn't receive much respect.

ESPN magazine was at the same University of Virginia football camp Billy attended, and they were following Marcus Vick, the younger brother of NFL star Michael Vick, for an upcoming magazine story. The younger Vick was a star recruit at the camp, and they wrote in their August 2001 edition of ESPN magazine:

"Unlike the deep talent pool of passers, the wide-out crop here is weak. There is Hill and Jesse Pellet-Rosa, a taller, less-refined kid, and Billy Gaines, a five-foot-seven Smurf who ran a 4.25 forty at the Penn State Nike combine (where the practice field runs slightly downhill). Virginia might offer a ride to two wide-outs, but probably not from this group."

That was typical of how Billy was treated during the recruiting process, except by Pittsburgh, who told him from the beginning they weren't worried about his size. I was disappointed that Virginia didn't seem to take Billy seriously, but I believe it added a little fuel to his belly. It just made him more determined to work hard.

His confidence seemed to grow. He seemed to take the rejection as motivation. He definitely had that underdog attitude that I believe pushed him to work and compete at a higher level. His confidence never wavered.

About a month after attending the Virginia camp, Billy said to a sports reporter, "You will get turned down more than accepted, so let it all add fuel to your fire. Never get down, and you will not be defeated. Fear no one, and always believe you are the best."

BLOOD on a Pew

We were disappointed that the scholarship offers weren't coming in. I understood the concern about his height, but I would turn on the television and see football players Billy's size playing all the time—even in the NFL. But he seemed to have a real hard time overcoming the height issue.

Billy felt a little discriminated against. Maybe it wasn't just his height that was holding him back.

As his father, I couldn't understand the problem. My son ran fast enough, jumped high enough, and was strong enough to play college football, so why wasn't he qualified?

It was more than being too short.

One of my favorite NFL coaches, former Indianapolis Colts head coach Tony Dungy, one of a handful of black head coaches in the NFL at the time, made a statement to the Orlando Sentinel in September of 2004 that may explain one of the reasons why my son wasn't receiving scholarship offers:

"You've got guys in high school, white players, who are discouraged from being wide receivers, defensive backs, or running backs—I think we do have that. It's 'This position is a white position' or 'black position.' I definitely believe (players) are channeled early on."

Billy played baseball in high school too, but his true passion was football. When he told one of the baseball coaches he was thinking about dropping baseball and concentrating on football, the coach made a comment that stuck with Billy, "You're not even five-feet-eight; you're not going far in football."

6: Football-A Lesson in Life

The baseball coach was right about one thing; Billy never made it to five-feet-eight. There was a board in the basement, where we measured him almost every month, from sixth grade until his junior year in high school. We laughed about it after he received his scholarship, but we were both so worried about his height or lack of. It took until about his junior year before he accepted the fact that he was going to be short.

High school football was the first step to overcoming the height stigma. Urbana High School was a new school, opening in the fall of 1996, coming off its first full season with a senior class. They had just completed an undefeated season and their first state championship in the fall of 1998. They had one of the best coaching staffs in the state, led by head coach Dave Carruthers and defensive coordinator Rick Conner, who went on to win a couple state championships as head coach of crosstown rival Linganore High School.

In addition to an undefeated season and strong coaches, the Hawks were stacked with several college-bound players, including starting quarterback and Penn State recruit Zack Mills. No question, having Zack back there tossing the ball around helped Billy grow and mature as a football player his sophomore season. Working in practice and playing in games with college-caliber recruits pushed Billy, and there were many college-bound football players on that roster over Billy's four years at Urbana.

Zack witnessed that underdog attitude first hand, and this is how he described it.

BLOOD on a Pew

The thing I remember about Billy is he was one of the hardest-working people you'll ever meet," Mills said. "I think he walked around thinking that he always had something to prove because of his size. Because of that, he worked so much harder than the average person.

I remember the first year I was at Penn State, whenever I'd come home, he'd always try to get in touch with me to get me to go out and throw with him. I don't get home that much, maybe a couple weeks out of the year, so the last thing I'd want to do is go throw. I wanted to relax, play golf or something. I think after a year and a half, he got the point. But we did go out and throw a couple of times.

Zack went on to have a fine career at Penn State where he wore the same t-shirt under his game uniform. It was a "Hometown Hero" t-shirt with Billy's high school number two and Gaines on the back to honor his deceased teammate.

Billy was on a team that seemed destined for greatness. Urbana high school went on to complete a state record of fifty consecutive wins with four state titles during that incredible run. Billy was fortunate enough to play in thirty seven of those games and catch the winning touchdown in their fourth straight state championship game for a one-point 7–6 victory winning number fifty at University of Maryland's Byrd stadium against a very tough Patuxent High School team.

6: Football-A Lesson in Life

That high school success did not come as easy at the next level. Football at the University of Pittsburgh started out mostly frustrating for Billy. They never got to see that 4.22 speed on the field, and Billy's unimpressive 4.9 yards per punt return earned him the nickname "Billy No-gains" by the Pittsburgh media his freshman season.

Billy wasn't going to give any excuses for his low return average. When asked about his punt return problems by the media, Billy said, "We definitely have the athletes on the punt team to do some special things. It is hard to say why it is not clicking yet. I put most of the blame on myself right now. I'm trying to gain some experience because I know that I have made a lot of mistakes, but I am just trying to correct some things. That first step is so important, and it is something I'm working on. If you can break that first defender, you usually have an opening to get at least twenty yards until the next wave of tackles come. You have to be a little crazy to do it because you get banged up so much, but I love that contact. In fact, I look for that contact. I love to get hit, and I have no fear back there. That's a good start. I know I'm close to breaking one, and frankly, I feel like I have what it takes to be a great one."

I flew out to South Bend with a friend to watch Pittsburgh play Notre Dame during Billy's freshman season on October 12, 2002. I wasn't planning to go; after all, we would have had another opportunity to watch Billy play at Notre Dame in a couple of seasons, so I thought. But my friend persisted, and we decided to fly out there to watch the game.

BLOOD on a Pew

It was the seventh game that season, and Pittsburgh was riding a 5–1 record into Notre Dame. It was a sloppy uneventful game where Billy didn't get many opportunities to make plays, and Pittsburgh lost a low-scoring game of 14–6. Afterwards, we met Billy as he was leaving the stadium to board the team bus. I tried to make lighthearted comments to ease the tension. "Hey look! It's Touchdown Jesus," I said as I pointed over to "The Word of Life Mural" of Jesus holding His arms up, but Billy barely spoke a word or cracked a grin. He was very disappointed in the team's close defeat and his lack of production as a punt returner. He was extremely frustrated and in no mood to talk.

There was one thing that came out of that dreary day at Notre Dame. Somebody snapped a picture of Billy being smothered by four Notre Dame players during one of his punt returns. Amazingly, two football seasons later, that same photo ended up on the cover of every Notre Dame Game Day magazine and game ticket when Pittsburgh was back in South Bend on November 13, 2004.

The team discovered the photo before the game, and they talked about it in the locker room. The players and coaches felt Billy was watching them play that day, and the Panthers went out inspired. In an exciting high-scoring, back and forth battle, the Panthers upset the highly-favored twenty-fourth ranked Fighting Irish by a score of 41–38 for Pitt's first win at South Bend since 1986. Coach Harris held up the program at his postgame news conference and said, "This young man being tackled here, he died in what was an unfortunate situation,

6: Football–A Lesson in Life

but he was with us today, and our football team dedicated this victory to him. He gave us the extra impetus to get the job done."

Pitt quarterback Tyler Palko, from the same recruiting class as Billy and Fitzgerald, didn't have those two guys to throw to that day as Larry went pro in 2004. Palko threw five touchdown passes and totaled 334 yards with no interceptions against Notre Dame, becoming the first opposing quarterback to throw for five touchdowns in a single game as a visiting team player against the Fighting Irish. Late in the fourth quarter, the Panthers went on two late scoring drives—one for a touchdown and one for a game-winning field goal with one second left to play.

An emotional Palko expressed what Billy's picture on the cover of every game day program and every ticket in the stadium meant to the Pitt football team:

"Billy always made us smile, and today, seeing that picture reminded us of what he meant, and we wanted to do the same for him. I know we did, and I know he is smiling, because there is no doubt he was looking down on us and watching this game."

Perhaps Billy was on the field that day. Less than two years after my son's death, I had felt like he was already forgotten, but this was a powerful reminder that he will never be forgotten—not by the people who loved and respected him.

Maybe Billy wasn't blessed with time to be an impact player at the University of Pittsburgh. He never got to see his sophomore season. But that day at Notre Dame, his legacy certainly left an impact on his coaches and teammates.

There was no question Billy's freshman year was challenging. I think he had realistic expectations going into his freshman season, but even with those expectations, things were tough.

The schedule was tough with teams like Notre Dame, Texas A&M, Virginia Tech, and Miami, to mention a few. But competition is what attracted Billy to Pittsburgh.

The competition for playing time was also difficult at a school known as "Wide Receiver U." The coaches were tough, as this was their livelihoods, and if the team lost, the coaches could eventually lose their jobs, and some players could lose their scholarship. Most kids go into college football with high expectations and Billy was no exception, but it can be a cold hard business. Practices were demanding, and classes were draining, but that's the life of a student athlete.

Billy was hurt in practice when a defensive back stepped on his foot and broke it. He missed the last few games including the bowl game because of the injury. Playing time was very limited his freshman season, and he knew that every year, new recruits were coming in to compete for his scholarship.

When I think back as to why Billy committed to play football at the University of Pittsburgh, it came down to who wanted Billy as a person and a football player more than anyone else did. He felt respected by the Pittsburgh coaching staff. With that respect, he thought he would

6: Football–A Lesson in Life

have the best opportunity to get on the field and play at Pittsburgh.

When the media asked Billy why he chose Pitt, he said, "It was the way Pitt treated me when I was there. Plus, I think it's an up-and-coming program. I think they're going to be real good in a few years." This was confirmed when Pitt made it to the BCS Tostitos Fiesta Bowl four seasons after Billy made that statement. It would have been his junior season.

There are certain plays that stick in my memory. One was his last play during the University of Pittsburgh team scrimmage game in the spring of 2003. The pass was high and deep and sailed for what seemed like forty yards or more before coming down into the left corner of the end zone. Billy had a couple steps on the defensive back, and the football floated right over his shoulder and into his arms. He snagged the ball and came down with both feet in the end zone before rolling to the ground.

Touchdown!

It was his first college touchdown. He bounced off the ground holding the ball and raising his hand and leaped into a teammate's arms. Even though it was just a spring game, it had to feel great.

The catch was later shown during an ESPN "Game Day" episode that fall while they did a short segment about Pitt receiver Larry Fitzgerald and the painful loss of his mother to cancer the previous spring. Larry shared the shock he experienced over Billy's death, and ESPN played a close-up of Billy's spring game touchdown grab. A touchdown grab that turned out to be his last catch.

7: Forgiveness

> Do not judge, and you will not be judged. Do not condemn, and you will not be condemned. Forgive, and you will be forgiven.
>
> Luke 6:37

It was May of 2009 and my wife Kim and I were attending the 40th annual fundraising and graduation ceremony banquet for the Frederick Rescue Mission. Kim's youngest brother, James, who struggled with alcoholism for most of his life, turned, looked at Kim, and said, "I need to ask you two something." He said this as we were saying our good-byes after an uplifting night of witnessing eight middle-aged men, including James, complete a twelve-month Christian-based drug and alcohol recovery program.

James pointed over to one of the men in the room and said, "See that guy over there? Pastor King preached on

7: Forgiveness

forgiveness. Have you two forgiven the priest who gave Billy alcohol?"

Without hesitation, Kim replied, "No!"

James never looked over at me for my response, and maybe it was a good thing, because my heart stopped, and I was speechless. It wasn't Kim's honest response that shocked me. I knew firsthand the anger she harbored in her soul.

But that question at the end of such a spirit-filled Christian celebration caught me totally off guard. James acted as if he anticipated Kim's response and that it confirmed something in his heart. He said, "Okay, I was just curious."

And that was that.

But the question bothered me as we drove home. Why did James ask such a question at a time like that? We were celebrating his newfound freedom as a Christian. Kim didn't seem to think twice about her response, but it troubled me, and the question tormented my conscience as I struggled to sleep that night.

What about everything else James heard over the last twelve months? I believe Kim's youngest brother looked at us as true Christians, and now he had an example of two Christians who don't forgive, or perhaps can't forgive.

James never looked for my response to his question on forgiveness. I was ready to answer, so I thought. At one point, I mumbled, "I have forgiven." But it was quiet and weak. He never heard it, and I didn't have the conviction to make sure he did.

How could I forgive the priest for supplying alcohol to my teenage son when my wife couldn't? Did she love Billy more than I did? Was she therefore angrier and hurt more deeply by his death?

I don't think you can compare a father's grief over the loss of his child to a mother's grief over the loss of her child. They are both deep and intense, but in some ways they can be different. My wife and I grieve very differently. Grief can be very unique in itself.

In the midst of my grief, I had become combative towards the Catholic church and in some ways judgmental towards Catholicism. Perhaps I developed a deep-rooted vendetta. I would be kidding myself if I didn't admit to anger. The reality is that I was angry...very angry.

I was angry with anybody and everybody who could have prevented this tragedy, including myself for not protecting my son. Eventually, however, my anger became focused squarely on the Catholic Church.

At times, it was almost a callous anger. It was as if God had forced me into a battle I never asked for, yet there I stood, face to face with a dilemma I never imagined. My family and I had to make some very tough choices, and they had to be made with the help of God.

A *Pittsburgh Tribune* writer attempted to expose us as weak and perhaps naïve for "astoundingly approving the plea agreement enabling the priest to walk away virtually scot-free." And perhaps he was right for calling us out like that. When asked why we agreed to "a slap on the wrist," or "more of a manicure, a hand massage" for the

7: Forgiveness

man guilty of supplying the alcohol and exposing Billy to the crawlspace that together would prove to be fatal, the only reasons I could come up with for agreeing with such leniency was the avoidance of a long, emotional trial, the fear of not getting a guilty verdict, and the concern that if the priest did go to jail, he might suffer the same fate as John Geoghan, the defrocked Boston priest and convicted child molester who was murdered in prison.

The Roman Catholic priest, Reverend Henry Krawczyk, was sentenced to seven years of probation and one hundred hours of community service for his part in Billy's death, a soft "slap on the wrist" for sure after pleading guilty to involuntary manslaughter and reckless endangerment. Had Krawczyk been convicted, he could have gone to prison for up to five years.

After an exhaustive and thorough criminal investigation exposing the fifty-year-old priest's history of supplying alcohol and preying on teenagers as far back as the mid- 1980's and of being transferred from parish to parish throughout the 80's and 90's, the evidence was overwhelming. However, after discussing it with our attorneys, we decided to accept a guilty plea bargain. We believed the trial would have been too hard on our family and friends, and at the end of the day, a guilty verdict for the more serious charge of involuntary manslaughter was a long shot, at best. We decided it wasn't worth the risk when a guilty plea was an admission of guilt and hopefully a strong message.

With a civil suit still pending, of course, Krawczyk was guarded with what he could say at the criminal plea hearing. Perhaps that's why he didn't accept responsibility or apologize. Even the judge acted as if he were disturbed by the pre-sentencing agreement that we approved.

But my question was, *Why were we asked in the first place?*

Should the punishment really be the decision of the victim's family, or should the punishment fit the crime? We were trying to follow our attorneys advice who, rightfully so, was concerned about our civil suit at the time.

We were perceived as showing mercy, but truthfully, at that time it was my angry and hurt wife who was actually more concerned for the safety of the man she believed killed her son.

It was the grieving mother who had grace and mercy in her heart during that difficult time. My focus wasn't on the wellbeing of the priest, I was still trying to make sense of something that I would eventually have to let go and trust God with.

After all the advice from our legal council, it came down to what we believe God wanted us to do. Would it have mattered if Krawczyk spent time in jail and absolutely nothing changed? Would the priest receiving a multi-year prison sentence have made a difference to anything or anybody?

We will never know if jail time would have made a difference, and I have to accept my responsibility for my part in that decision. But it is important to point out that everything about the case was exposed in the newspapers many times over—particularly the issue of the Pittsburgh Diocese not keeping more careful records of,

7: Forgiveness

if not a closer eye on Krawczyk after receiving complaints that he'd served alcohol to minors. He should have been under serious surveillance after the first complaint.

But like many allegations of serious misconduct toward minors involving Catholic clergy that was just beginning to come out, this one slipped through the cracks as well.

Because of all the media coverage from the trial and civil suit, I felt the filth was exposed. Now how do they clean it up? My family went through hell during their part in unmasking the evil, and now it was up to the Catholic Church to take a long, hard look in the mirror and recognize that enlarging plank entrenched from its eye.

In that same *Pittsburgh Tribune* article, the writer asked me how realistic my concern was about Krawczyk's safety if he were to go to prison, given that most prisoners probably wouldn't consider Krawczyk's offense nearly as grievous as Geoghan's crimes and because of that, Krawczyk would probably be safe. I tried to answer him as honestly as I possibly could, but I don't believe I made my point. The question he posed was interesting, and I did pause before answering. I was quoted as saying:

"I don't like to compare calamity. I don't like to compare the abuse of hundreds of innocent souls to blood on a pew. There probably would be some prisoners in there who wouldn't care what Krawczyk had done. They would still harm him." Actually, I was misquoted and didn't think much of it at the time, but I actually said, "The abuse of thousands of innocent souls." I was referring to the world wide clergy sex abuse scandal that was still coming out at the time and not Geoghan's child sex abuse crimes. I was trying to make a point about the magnitude of the problem and the possibility that some prisoners could associate Kwawczyk with child abusers. I don't believe I got my point across.

There was a watershed study released by the US Catholic leaders in 2005 on the clergy sex abuse crisis, finding that 10,667 minors had been abused by 4,392 clerics since 1950.

I wished I had rephrased the writer's question to what I really heard him ask me that day. In other words, was the death of my nineteen-year-old son in a Catholic Church less deplorable than the sexual abuse of hundreds of innocent children in a Catholic Church? Why am I asked such a question?

Why was my family put in that brutal predicament? A Christian man falls to his death in a Catholic Church and bleeds on their pew, and the spotlight came down on his dead, broken body which illuminated a history of corruption in the church hierarchy, exposing its sin to the world. The spotlight eventually shifted to the surviving family, and now we had to act, and we had to have God's guidance.

So after much prayer, we decided to hire a powerful Washington, DC law firm and file a wrongful death suit, not only against the priest, but also against the Diocese of Pittsburgh for $75 million for their part in Billy's death. We felt a sense of responsibility to make a statement

7: Forgiveness

about the gross negligence within the leadership of the Catholic Church in Pittsburgh.

I never believed we were suing the church. We were filing a wrongful death suit against the evil that infiltrated and exposed the church, and hopefully doing our part to help minimize the possibility of future tragedies within the church.

I felt it was a risk—not because I thought we would lose. I knew we had a strong case. The risk was much deeper than the strength of the case. The risk was in God's will.

Did God want us to sue the Catholic Church?

If I hadn't believed that this was what God wanted us to do, that it was our responsibility and God's will, we never would have sued. If I hadn't believed God wanted us to make a statement and hopefully make a difference by directing attention to a secret that had to be revealed, we would have handled things differently.

To me, this was God's way of uncovering a wrong that needed to be confronted. I don't claim to know why Billy had to die, but the fact is he died by falling to his death in a Catholic Church sanctuary after being served alcohol by their priest, and now it seemed that God was placing this responsibility on Billy's family to act.

I do worry about what God thinks, and I'm well-aware of His blessing and His wrath. Other people will judge me regardless of what I do or don't do, and there will always be misunderstandings in this world. Perception is reality in this world, but truth is reality from heaven.

There are no misunderstandings with God. I can't fool Him and He knows my every thought. He knows what I do in private, and he knows my thoughts in public. God knows my motive for filing the wrongful death lawsuit, and I had to look in the mirror and make sure my motive was Gods will, for it is God that we all must ultimately stand before. It is God who is the ultimate judge.

We never expected to see the full $75 million, and we knew it was an attention-getter and we would receive both positive and negative attention. But it was reported at the time that the Catholic Church had already spent at least $657 million to settle abuse lawsuits. Was our lawsuit going to make a difference? Would people be callous by then and barely notice our drop-in-the-bucket case? Would people be cynical by then and only see the money, only see the victims as seeking money?

Eventually, we knew we would get some kind of monetary settlement, and the question was, W*hat then? What purpose does money play in this tragedy?* Of course, we would rather be homeless and on the street and have our son back than have all the riches in the world and not have him here with us, but that wasn't a choice. We were forced to act, and we believed it was God's will.

So it was time. After about two and half years of going back and forth with the settlement offers, feeling many times like we were trying to put a price tag on our dead son's toe, we were faced with a decision. It was time to put this chapter behind us and try to move forward. We agreed to settle, and that battle ended.

But the battle to forgive continued.

7: Forgiveness

The Bible makes it very clear; we are commanded to forgive. In Matthew 6:15. Jesus said, "But if you don't forgive others, your Father will not forgive your sins."

I know I need God's forgiveness, but what makes forgiving others so difficult? Sin such as anger and pride, which can eat you alive.

The problem I have with apologies is that I never know how sincere the person actually is. But the truth is, if I know God knows exactly how sincere a person's heart is, my concern needs to be on my heart and forgiveness. God knows how sincere my heart is as well.

I haven't received many apologies in my life, and perhaps there are a few people I felt owed me one, including the priest and the Catholic Church for not removing the troubled priest before my son had to die. But had they been offered, would I have accepted them as sincere?

I don't know.

But does God require they ask my forgiveness? My forgiveness must come without being asked to forgive.

The truth is I don't know that they believe they have anything for which to be forgiven. My forgiveness must come from my heart, and I must obey the One who commands it and be aware of the One who knows my heart.

C.S. Lewis wrote, "Everyone says forgiveness is a lovely idea, until they have something to forgive." Forgiving the priest and the Catholic Church has been extremely difficult. It's a lifelong process. It takes faith to forgive. I don't know if I could forgive without the help of God. I had to have faith that God would be just. It takes trust to forgive. I had to trust that I was doing God's will by forgiving. It wasn't enough for me to forgive because it may help me feel better. I had to forgive because I love God, and it is His commandment.

Renowned Christian author and theologian Lewis Smedes wrote, "To forgive is to set a prisoner free and discover that the prisoner was you."

God knew what he was doing by giving me that most difficult command. It humbled me and forced me to look into the mirror. The person staring back didn't have to squint too hard to see that huge wooden plank sticking out of the side of his eye. No—I didn't want to forgive, and I certainly hated looking into the mirror and seeing that ugly plank.

The choice to forgive is an act of the will, or an act against your will, but more importantly, forgiveness is God's will.

I can remember someone coming up to me just days after the settlement and congratulating me. He said, "I know that's what you wanted." I cringed at first, as I realized that he wasn't alone in that perception. I didn't have a response because I really didn't know how to respond.

No, it wasn't what I wanted. I wanted my son back.

I wanted my son's life to have meaning. I wanted his tragic death used to make a difference. I wanted to do God's will. Perhaps that's what he meant by "what I wanted."

We are forbidden to disclose the terms of our settlement with the Catholic Church. There is no amount of money in this world that can compensate for the loss of a child. The money was never the point. From the begin-

7: Forgiveness

ning, I felt that the money would have no meaning unless there was positive change. The money was meaningless unless we can give back in some way over time, over a lifetime. We are nothing more than stewards of God's money regardless of where the money comes from. Unless we use God's money to ultimately bring Him glory, then we've missed the boat. Money is no more than an instrument or tool that can do great harm or great good to the kingdom of God.

It isn't money that is the "root of all evil;" it's the "love of money" that 1 Timothy 6:10 describes as the "root of all evil."

It hasn't been easy since the settlement, and if I were to die today, I would fear I failed as a good steward in God's eyes. If I were to die today, I believe I would not have had time in this life to be a good steward of God's money.

As long as I have breath, I will try to be a better steward of His money, of His world, of His blessings, but there will be battles.

But the battle's not over for me yet.

I can't help but feel like God is sending me a personal message when things seem so incredibly difficult. Maybe the worldwide recession, credit crunch, housing crisis, auto crisis, bank crisis, and historic market crash weren't directed specifically at me, but it certainly felt like it at times. I'm not privy to why my family experienced gut wrenching tragedies over the past few years but the timing of these tragedies definitely tested my faith.

The truth is God's blessing is pouring out on us every day, and we're too distracted by this world to realize it. To have a healthy family and a good marriage is a blessing. Being alive, having more time in this world and living in America, free to write this story, is yet another incredible blessing. To have a peace in my heart that can only come from heaven is a blessing beyond words. To wake up each morning and recognize God's grace in my life is an answered prayer. To have family and friends that truly love me is an underserved gift. I could go on and on about how truly blessed I am when I step back and open my eyes through the lenses of eternity.

It's as if God threw open the floodgates of heaven and poured out so much blessing upon me that I'm incapable of receiving it all at once.

8: Moving Forward

"My grace is sufficient for you, for my power is made perfect in weakness."

2 Corinthians 12:9

Right after Billy's death, perhaps for the first time in my life, God had my full, undivided attention. I believe C.S. Lewis described it best when he wrote, "God whispers to us in our pleasures, speaks in our conscience, but shouts in our pains. It's a megaphone to rouse a deaf world."

It was almost four years after Billy's death and seven months after burying my father, who died at 68 years old on July 29th 2006, after a six month battle with cancer.

I stood in the lobby of the hospital waiting to talk to the doctors about my youngest son Nicholas, who was in critical but stable condition.

He was the driver in a tragic auto accident that killed his friend Tyler.

BLOOD on a Pew

The hospital scene with Nick in Baltimore was definitely different, but it was equally harrowing and eerily similar to the scene in Pittsburgh. Friends and family had their Saturday plans interrupted and made the trek to the hospital in downtown Baltimore, and there was a lot of concern for Nick's survival.

We were all aware of one death, and Nicholas was far from out of the woods. Pastor Guy and a few other members of our church gathered the large group in the waiting area and led us in prayer. We prayed aloud, and I can remember the difference I felt as I prayed for Nicholas. With Billy, it was about praying for a miracle. He was clinically brain-dead, and it would have taken a true miracle to bring him back, but we prayed anyway. With Billy's situation, it was about surviving, our survival. He was gone, and unless we were going to see a miracle, we would have to survive without him.

Perhaps survival was the miracle.

One could say our prayers went unanswered with Billy, or answered with a resounding no, but we can't see everything God sees, and we don't have all the answers. I have survived along with a stronger renewed sense of faith. That was obvious as we prayed for my youngest son nearly four years later.

With Nick's situation, I was overwhelmed and humbled by how much faith filled the waiting room. God wants us to pray with the faith of a child. We all knew Billy wasn't blessed with a miracle recovery, even though we prayed with all our hearts, pleaded with all our souls, and begged with tears in our eyes to no avail.

8: Moving Forward

Maybe I was worried that since we were disappointed once, perhaps there would be a whimper of a prayer, a prayer with less breath or spirit, a weaker prayer, a passionless plea for help. It was as if we got our breath knocked out with Billy, and we all knew God's will would be done in Nick's situation as well. We couldn't change God's mind. Yet the prayers were just as confident in knowing God was listening and just as humble in knowing His will would be done and we would accept it either way. We prayed with the knowledge that God loves prayer. He listens, He cares, He acts, and it can change the world.

Nick would have several surgeries over the coming months to repair his broken back with rods and his broken collarbone with screws. He went to jail for a year of his life, and now he lives with the life sentence of his friend's death.

Though we were blessed to have Nicholas back, we grieved over Nicholas and the loss of his best friend Tyler. As parents who know the pain of losing a child, we mourned over watching our son go to jail for the horrible crime of crashing his truck and causing the death of another parents child. It's been very difficult to write about. There is a numbness that settles in over me as I type those words.

As a father who lost a son, I had to ask that question I think many parents are confronted with after losing a child. Was my son's death in vain? Billy's accident should have served as a warning to others about the dangers of intoxication and the consequences of peer pressure. The shocking reality was, after seeing the reaction to Nick's accident, Billy's death was used as an excuse for his grief stricken younger brothers poor decisions that horrific night. So not only did Billy's tragic death not serve as a warning, it was blamed for more drinking, more risky behavior, more destruction, and, ultimately, more death.

How did God feel as He watched me all those years live my life basically ignoring the death of His son? Perhaps living my life as if His son had died in vain? My expressions of gratitude in my prayers for spoiling me with the comforts of this world, for blessing me with a nice home, secure job, and a healthy family, weren't followed by actions of appreciation. In many ways, I lived as if I had God's favor, and perhaps I believed I deserved it, because after all, wasn't I basically a good person? But it wasn't about me being a good person. Good by whose standards, whose definition, whose opinion? Is anybody really good enough to enter God's presence? Can anybody work their way into heaven? Was my faith considered dead in the eyes of God?

I was an honest person and watched my language for the most part. I was friendly and always tried to wave cheerfully to my neighbors as I drove down the street. I worked hard to support my family and attend all of my kids' sporting events as much as possible. But was that good enough? What did I really deserve?

I never really got it. I had blinders on and could only see what was in front of me. Even as I write this last chapter, I know I have a long way to go. I felt so blessed that I didn't need the rest. I felt so blessed by God that my spiritual senses for depending on Him actually

8: Moving Forward

became dull and callous. I became so comfortable and content with my life that I lost the reality of why I'm alive. I became so comfortable in my blessings that I forgot the One who blesses. I took God and everything He represents for granted.

As I was going through Billy's stuff, I picked up that little brown book he was reading while staying at the convent—*The Screwtape Letters* by one of my favorite authors, C.S. Lewis. There was a short note inside the book cover, and I could see it was a high school graduation gift from Billy's youth pastor in Maryland.

Lewis published *The Screwtape Letters* in 1942 as a series of thirty-one letters written by a senior demon named Screwtape to his nephew, a young demon named Wormwood. Screwtape's letters to his nephew contain advice for how to turn Wormwood's "patient," an ordinary man living in war-time England, toward "their Father below" (Satan or the devil) and away from "their Enemy" (God or Christ).

When I opened *The Screwtape Letters* for the first time, I started reading through chapter eight as if it were dog-eared for a reason. I believe it was.

Chapter eight starts with the senior demon, Screwtape, explaining to the young demon, Wormwood, that low points or "troughs" in a person's life are used by God more than the good times or the "peaks" to get "permanent possession" of a person's soul.

Screwtape also tells Wormwood in chapter eight that it is during these hard times, "the troughs," that people turn to God and seek His will, much more so than during the good times.

The senior demon instructs the junior demon to recognize God's will in drawing souls to Him during times of grief or hardships, and then do the opposite.

Screwtape concludes chapter eight with a compelling warning to his demon apprentice. An attitude that this book illuminates throughout. As believers, we are to live our lives to disappoint the enemy, to be aware that there is an evil cause or purpose to keep us off track, or, if we are on track, derail us from the truth. There is an invisible battle for our souls and we need to recognize it. Here is Screwtape's warning at the end of chapter eight: "Do not be deceived Wormwood. Our cause is never more in danger than when a human, no longer desiring, but still intending, to do our Enemy's will, looks round upon a universe from which every trace of Him seems to have vanished, and asks why he has been forsaken, and still obeys."

That moment for me was when I climbed back through the window and walked by the crawlspace, the short ladder caught my attention. I paused; *What was it that drew Billy into that creepy, dark crawlspace?* I thought to myself as we walked by. If Billy was "miraculously spared" from the house fire, why wasn't he saved from this crawlspace?

The words of Jesus on the cross echoed in my mind. "My God, My God, why have you forsaken Me?"

I also knew at that moment I was at a crossroads in my faith. I never truly believed I was forsaken by God.

8: Moving Forward

It was really the opposite. I felt His presence as I stood at the end of the crawlspace. I wasn't privy to why God allowed Billy to fall to his death. But what I was privy to was Gods unlimited love and boundless grace. And now I was confronted with a rather profound question. How much did I love God? My answer to that question would have everything to do with the road I would ultimately take.

As I read these letters from this book through the years after Billy's death, I discovered a scary truth about my life. I could have been the "patient" in the book. In many ways, I lived my life oblivious to Satan and his attacks. I was focused on the earthly world and was easily distracted by its hidden, subliminal allure. I didn't recognize myself as under spiritual attack, and if someone tried to point it out, I don't think I would have taken them seriously.

This is right out of the book where Lewis has the old devil instruct his apprentice in this very matter:

> "My dear Wormwood, I wonder you should ask me whether it is essential to keep the patient in ignorance of your own existence. That question, at least for the present phase of the struggle, has been answered for us by the High Command. Our policy, for the moment, is to conceal ourselves."

For most of my life, I was oblivious to the power of this "concealed" spiritual enemy. I was unaware of the continuous sneak attacks on my life, and I was in serious danger. How could I recognize an attack of this evil magnitude without being shocked into reality? The plan was being executed in such a deep, dark, methodical manner. For me, this evil adversary became reality. I began to recognize the enemy that lurks in the spiritual realm and how effective his tactics can be. It was as if the curtain was pulled, and they scurried away like frightened rats. I had to be on guard against these subtle, yet eternally dangerous attacks of the mind.

Prior to Billy's death, my faith and relationship with God were private. In many ways, I would have considered myself an undercover or closet Christian. In some ways, I was probably ashamed of my faith. Though I was a Christian for most of my life, I felt like a lifelong member of the "invisible church." Very private and extremely independent, I lived a seemingly self-reliant life, with faith as my invisible security blanket of sorts. I prayed for protection over my family and myself and felt safe and secure. I felt blessed, and truly protected by God.

It was just me and God.

Though I attended church on occasion, I didn't always feel like I truly fit in. It seemed like I was always looking for a different church. We did finally settle on a church, but even then, I would get this unsettling urge to shop around, perhaps find a church that offered more, perhaps a church with more entertainment and less obligation. I might disagree with something in the sermon or take the message as a direct assault. Maybe I would sense coolness from someone in the congregation or from a leader in the church. It didn't matter; I was focused on the wrong thing. My faith and trust were in other people, and even-

8: Moving Forward

tually, I would always be disappointed and off on a new church hunt.

C.S. Lewis has his senior demon, Screwtape; describe this same attitude in *The Screwtape Letters*.

> Surely you know that if a man can't be cured of churchgoing, the next best thing is to send him all over the neighborhood looking for the church that "suits" him until he becomes a taster or connoisseur of churches.

I certainly was in danger of becoming a "connoisseur of churches," and I definitely didn't believe church attendance was God's priority for me at the time. But what was God looking for from me?

Things aren't always what they seem... and I'm reminded of that every day.

I respected a few famous athletes and coaches through the years, and perhaps one of the biggest, toughest football players I had ever watched play the game was the late Reverend Reggie White. The former Philadelphia Eagle and Green Bay Packer Hall of Fame defensive end spoke publically about his Christian faith many times and was nicknamed the "Minister of Defense." Yet, I believe part of me felt like religion and church was for the weak or for women and children. Perhaps I thought I was a little too cool or strong for church and religion. After all, what was my true motive for attending church? Did I want God's blessing? Did I think if my wife and kids went and I went as well, life could be easier? Wasn't that a good enough reason? I mean after all, it had to be good for the kids to go, but I certainly didn't need it... so I thought.

Where did this deception come from? After all, I was a believer, but there is no other way to describe it; deception!

Perhaps my heart was a little callous and cool towards the very place and people it should have been the most loving and warm—other Christians, other believers, the church, and its family.

Dare I say, I could have been perceived as a "lukewarm Christian" by other believers? I could have been viewed as "lukewarm" by the opinion that matters the most: God's view. Was I living like that person described in Revelation 3:16? "Because you are lukewarm—neither hot nor cold—I am about to spit you out of my mouth."

Was I walking spit in the eyes of God?

I believe there are times when God wants us to look for another church or small group. But if I left a church or small group because somebody made a remark I didn't like or had an attitude I didn't agree with or just rubbed me the wrong way, I would never belong to any church. Yet the Bible makes it clear that I'm a citizen with God's people and a member of God's household.

"God's household." Is there a better way to describe the Christian church?

The Christian church really is a fellowship of imperfect, repenting sinners who are in the process of being sanctified by their faith in Christ, a process that takes a lifetime.

8: Moving Forward

I can live life to the fullest, regardless of my circumstance—not because life in this world is so wonderful (it's not) but because I discovered my true citizenship of another land—an everlasting citizenship in heaven.

I see the adversity in my life as a temporary setback and the painful experiences as an opportunity for spiritual insight and character building.

I live this life for what it truly is—a long, exciting journey or a short, painful adventure. Ultimately, they both lead to the same place: home. I can live life without worrying about what tomorrow's going to bring and knowing tomorrow is yet another day closer to eternity.

Since Billy's death, I have found the fellowship of other Christians extremely therapeutic and humbling in many ways. I have discovered how much God uses other people to communicate His purpose and His message, and I have learned over the years that God's church isn't made up of the brick building with the cross in front but the loving and caring people inside.

Over the past several years, I have grown to appreciate life just a little more. I have discovered how blessed I truly am. However, the word "blessed" has taken on a completely new meaning.

In Psalm 29:11, it says, "The Lord gives strength to his people; the Lord blesses his people with peace."

To me, to be truly blessed is to take my God given gift of strength and peace and share it with others. There is no doubt, to be a blessing to others is to glorify God and glorifying God is the reason humans were created in the first place.

BLOOD on a Pew

We are all hardwired for eternity, and our souls ache when we watch our loved ones leave this world. It could be a slow grueling exit or a flash. Either way, death hurts and the pain can linger for a lifetime.

The reality is, we are just a vapor or mist passing through for a short time. The truth is we could be gone with an exit so sudden it leaves our loved ones behind with a sense of unfinished business. Billy left this world with the cold, hard reality of death, but I was left behind to survive and move forward with a sense of truth that leads me to see life through God's lenses—the lenses of eternity.

I still pray for safety over my family, but there is no such thing as truly being safe in this dangerous world. This is a fallen world. Accidents occur every second somewhere. Physically or emotionally, people either get hurt or die with every blink. We live in a violent world where innocent people are murdered, raped, robbed, assaulted, and abused every day in incomprehensible numbers.

C.S. Lewis described this world as an "enemy-occupied territory."

We truly live in "enemy-occupied territory."

But there is true safety in another world. There is a place where "perfect safety" reigns and you have true protection from pain and death.

The words from the book *When God Weeps* by Joni Eareckson Tada and Steven Estes comes to mind when I think about the pain and suffering in this world.

"God permits what he hates to achieve what he loves."

8: Moving Forward

God hates death. Death is brutal and it can tear our heart out and leave us in utter despair when we lose someone we love. We put them in a box and close the door forever.

It is life that God loves and scripture makes it very clear, "He is the God of the living." He created us to live!

Yet we must go on living in a world where there are more dead than living. I live with a void in my heart. A missing piece to my family unit, and I'm reminded every time I get that urge to call or email or visit Billy. It's a constant reminder of my own mortality. I can almost hear the ticks of the clock get louder with each day. Yet I don't live in fear of death. My fear is not living to my fullest potential in the eyes of God.

It took the sudden death of my teenage son to wake me from my sense of worldly security and physical protection. Though, I believed I was a true born again or saved Christian since I was a teenager, it took the shock of burying my own teenage son for me to get the true meaning of the terms "born again' and "saved." It took the horrific death of my son in a church for me to comprehend the meaning and power behind the death of Jesus Christ on the cross and the meaning of the sacrifice. It took my son's blood to open my eyes to God's only son's blood.

When I grieved over Billy's death, I recognized the harrowing death of Jesus Christ on the cross and the unimaginable joy over Christ's resurrection and the message of hope it brings. Does anyone deserve hell more than a drunk mocker falling to his death on a church pew?

Perhaps I do, but scripture makes it very clear, because of the incomprehensible value of Jesus' blood on the cross, Billy's sins were forgiven, all of them, past, present and future, paid in full by that same Holy blood. Since Billy had repented and trusted Jesus Christ with his soul, he may have died a drunken sinner, but he entered paradise a precious saint in the eyes of God.

It's not always about how you die. Not many of us will die a heroic death.

The truth is nobody can live a sinless life. Romans 3:23 makes that very clear, "for all have sinned and fall short of the glory of God." If we need to live a sinless life to enter the kingdom of heaven—we're all doomed! Jesus was the only sinless person. He came down to earth so that He would be the perfect sacrifice to save us from hell. Now that is a heroic death!

Wouldn't it be offensive to God to believe the death of His son wasn't enough? That my sin was so bad that even the sacrifice of the savior of the world on the cross was inadequate? To actually think the death of Christ, who was God incarnate, was insufficient, wouldn't that diminish the value of the gospel? To believe more is required to cleanse us from all sin, to save us from eternal death, or that we can save ourselves, isn't that missing the core message of the gospel? Jesus Christ died and rose from the dead, so we may be saved.

1 Peter 3:18 says, "Christ suffered for our sins once for all time. He never sinned, but he died for sinners to bring you safely home to God. He suffered physical death, but he was raised to life in the Spirit."

8: Moving Forward

"Raised to life in the Spirit to bring you safely home to God." Is there any better description of eternity?

I view God's protection differently now. It is a powerful, eternal protection of the soul. His protection goes way beyond this world and is never about just protecting the body. The temporary nature of our life is but a flash. If we live to be a hundred, it's but a blink in the eyes of God.

God tugged at Billy's heart at a very young age. He responded by stepping up and stepping into the baptismal tub. At the young age of eleven, he decided it was time to be baptized. I never pushed it, discussed it, or even encouraged it. I was too distracted by life, and something like baptism could wait, so I thought. But Billy felt the sense of urgency; he felt the need to make a public statement, confirming his faith, not to get into heaven, but to show his love and commitment to Jesus Christ and to publicly pronounce his Christian faith.

As a father who lost a son, this is my way of letting Billy publicly pronounce his Christian faith from the grave. I know it's not what our greatest enemy Satan wants, but it's as if my dead son depends on me for his redemption and immortality—not because he was a hero or needs to be remembered. Billy didn't die a heroic death, but his death is being used by God, because it is the message of the gospel that needs to be remembered. It's the consequence of sin and the reality of death that needs to be recognized. It's the fact that it can happen to you or someone you love that we all should be aware of.

There was a price to be paid. There was a consequence for his actions. Intoxication cut Billy's life short. He didn't graduate from college and kiss his mother on the cheek on senior day. He didn't get married and have his own family. He missed it all. His time in this world was cut short, and he paid a hefty price. We paid a hefty price. But without a doubt, Billy's greatest loss was his time to fulfill his God given purpose in this world. Time is a gift from God; what we do with that time is our gift back to God.

I started a website about a year after Billy's death at www.BillyGaines.org. I have received several emails from young college athletes from all over the country who had been moved by the website and Billy's story. That is my motivation for writing this book. I'm completing a mission that was left incomplete. This is God's way of allowing Billy's life and death to serve a purpose that is far greater than playing football or being blamed for the destructive behavior of others.

What could be worse than leaving this world before finishing my purpose for being alive? What if after death, I find myself in the judgment seat of Christ with His work still left to be done through me? What would my excuse be? I believed, yet I didn't live like a believer. I had Christ in my heart, yet I was harnessed by worldly distractions. I had good intentions, yet I never got off the couch or I was just too busy. Perhaps I let the perception of others define who I was and what I would do. And the truth is God has blessed every believer with a special gift and we are to use that gift for His glory.

8: Moving Forward

Reading through the last book of the Bible, Revelations, I noticed one word kept appearing over and over again. It is a powerful word that I believe is meant to be in the last book of the Bible as many times as it is for a reason. The word "overcome" or "overcame" appears in the book of Revelation eleven times. There is no question—God wants us to overcome our hardships and despair we suffer in this world and to rejoice that we overcame by turning to Christ.

As written in Revelation 21:7 about eternity, "He who *overcomes* will inherit all this, and I will be his God and he will be my son."

God never promised a pain-free life. As a matter of fact, he guaranteed a life of trouble throughout scripture. One example in John 16:33, Jesus said, "I have told you these things, so that in me you may have peace. In this world you will have trouble. But take heart! I have overcome the world." There's that word again. It's a word I will always catch; the word "overcome" is a word that jumps from the page and grabs my heart.

In many ways I had to overcome myself before writing this story. I had to overcome my pride and insecurity. I had to overcome the world and turn to God for His will. My fear is leaving this world with regret. My fear is leaving this world with an incomplete or unfinished mission. I am afraid of missing the most important reason for being alive. I have to accept the gift of freedom and live the way my Creator designed me—free.

I poked my head out from my security and comfort zone and asked God to help me complete my pre-destined mission before I departed the battlefield. I asked God to protect my family and me in this dangerous world. I also asked God to use my family and me for His will and His purpose to help advance His kingdom and to bring glory to Him.

I believe God is answering that prayer as I move forward one day at a time. Perhaps in such a way I'm incapable of fully comprehending on this side of eternity.

My ascension from grief and despair began when I focused on another world. When I humbly looked up to seek God and His kingdom, I began to see another land as my true home. I began to see God as my true Father. I began to understand the value of my time in this world and like it says in John 8:32, "Then you will know the truth, and the truth will set you free."

I recognize the true enemy now, and he wants me to turn away from God. He wants me to be petty and bitter. He wants me to hold a grudge and harden my heart towards the Catholic Church. He wants me to resent my family and quarrel with my neighbor. He wants to fill me with rage and anger. He wants to fill me with pride and materialism. He wants to tempt me with sin and feed my mind with lies and lust. He wants me to feel haughty and too highly of myself. He wants me to fear and lose faith. He wants me depressed and distracted from what matters most. He wants me to be vindictive and turn away from the One who can save me. He wants to kill me, but it's not my body he's worried about.

The enemy's battle is ultimately for my soul.

8: Moving Forward

It's easy to find God when we believe He saved us from harm, or life is good, but it's when every trace of God seems to have vanished, that the words of Jesus on the cross echo through our soul. "My God, my God, why have You forsaken me?"

Just like Screwtape instructed his junior demon, it's when we turn to God during our darkest hour, that we do the most damage to Satan's plan and purpose for us. We turn and face our evil adversary whose sole purpose is to win our souls—we look him in the eyes and say two words. *You lose!*

Chucky Mullins, the University of Mississippi defensive back who broke his neck playing football was asked an interesting question the day he left the hospital in a wheelchair. "Is there a part of the Bible that is your favorite?" A news reporter shouted at the press conference.

His reply to that question comes back to me as I end my story.

"Yes," he replied. Then he quoted Philippians 4:13.

"I can do all things through Christ, which strengthens me."

Here was a kid who was paralyzed, stuck in a wheel chair, told he would be paralyzed for life, in his darkest hour, and yet, he knew exactly where to go for strength to endure.

Chucky Mullins wasn't bitter. He didn't understand why that freak accident happened to him, but he accepted it and turned to Christ for strength.

I find myself comforted by the words of this courageous young college football player and the verse he quoted.

I never could have moved forward and written this story without the power of Christ, who strengthens me daily.

It was my great-grandmother Myrtle, my grandmother Margie, and my mother, Joyce, who had the greatest spiritual impact in my life.

I can remember as a small boy catching my great-grandmother Myrtle reading her Bible by her nightstand before bed. She was a little woman with a big hug. She was a woman who experienced great love and great pain, losing a baby to sickness and a teenager to murder. Is there a greater spiritual warrior than a frail great-grandmother, reading her Bible after a life of surviving such pain and despair? Who does the enemy fear more? Her faith not only survived; it thrived.

My grandmother Margie also had a hard life. She was the firstborn of a large family, and when she was born, they thought she was dead, so they placed her in the snow. She awoke with a scream to let everybody know she was alive. She survived the death of her younger siblings, her husband, and a granddaughter who was sixteen and pregnant when she died from a brain aneurism. My grandmother always found a way to make me feel special. She wasn't well-educated, and she didn't have much money, but she was one of the most loving, caring people I knew. She could read me like a book and was always concerned about *others*. It was never about *her*.

8: Moving Forward

My sons' "Grammy," my mother, planted the seed of faith in all of us at a very young age. She spoke to us about God probably more than anybody else did in our lives. My mother's first-born died during delivery. She was only nineteen at the time. I believe her faith changed after that tragic event. My mother would know the pain of losing a grandchild as well. When I would catch my mom sharing her faith with my kids, it took me back thirty years. As a child, I can remember going to church occasionally, but God was always present in my life through my mother.

Billy's mother had a strong influence on his faith. To give you an idea of the heart of Billy's mother, here are some of her words as she wrestled with the indescribable grief of losing her son. She wrote these inspirational words of faith to God in her personal journal just weeks after burying her son.

She wrote,

> I need to lean on your Word for comfort, peace, guidance, and happiness. Because of You, I have reason to go on. You blessed me with three children, a wonderful husband, a loving family, dear friends, a good job, a nice home, health … the list is endless. But your greatest blessing to me is your promise of love, comfort, strength, happiness, eternal life, and the fact I will see my son again.

My wife struggles every day from the scars left behind, but that promise is seared deep into her soul, which carries her when she can't get up. God carries her every day.

Billy didn't consider himself a hero, but he expressed who he considered the true heroes in one of his last emails to me on March 21, 2003, less than three months prior to his death and shortly after the war in Iraq started.

He wrote, "I'm just trying to keep in mind how lucky I am compared to those eighteen- and nineteen-year olds across seas getting bullets fired at them."

Perhaps the biggest lesson I've learned over the past few years is the power of love and humility. Pain can drop you to your knees and humble you, and it takes humility to both receive grace and give grace.

Thank you for taking the time to ride my spiritual journey with me. I've asked God many questions throughout this story. And like Chucky Mullins said nearly twenty years ago after he broke his neck in a tackle, "I don't understand it, but I've accepted it."

In Proverbs 3:5 it says, "Trust in the Lord with all your heart and lean not on your own understanding."

There is so much about God that is incomprehensible, but I do believe His Word answers my question in this story. In 2 Corinthians 12:9, Jesus answered Paul's plea to remove "the thorn from his flesh," with these words.

"My grace is sufficient for you, for my power is made perfect in weakness."

To know God's grace is to understand it is indeed sufficient.

God's grace is His greatest gift to me. I certainly don't deserve it, and I could never earn it, for the very definition of grace is "the freely given, unmerited favor and love of God." His grace means that no sin I commit or mistake

8: Moving Forward

I make in this life can disqualify me from His promise of eternity. God's grace means I'm never beyond redemption, and I have no sin beyond forgiveness. Because of God's grace, I have survived the gut-wrenching grief and staggering blows over the past six years. Because of God's grace, I can be secure in knowing I will survive any heartache and hardships that may await me in the future. God's grace enables me to awake each day with a clean slate, filling my heart with faith, hope and meaning. It is by the grace of God I can see the fleeting nature of this life, yet live with the confidence of an everlasting future.

Though God shouted through a megaphone to get my attention; it was the whisper of the Holy Spirit that drew my heart closer to Him. As a brokenhearted parent, pouring over the Holy Bible, searching for answers, seeking the truth, desperate to understand the death of my son. God was speaking directly to me through His Word. There was no avoiding His love. It was from God, and I understood His message of eternity through grace and it changed my heart. It changed my life. I repented, and He forgave all of my sins. I trusted, and Jesus became my Savior and sealed my soul for eternity. I asked God to help me live a life of purpose, and He inspired me to write this book. Those powerful holy words of the Bible came directly from heaven—directly from the hand of God.

That same powerful yet loving hand caught my son's soul as he was falling from the ceiling of St. Anne's on that dreadful night.

BLOOD on a Pew

I don't visit Billy's gravesite very often, but when I do, I drop to one knee and say a quiet prayer. God loves our quiet personal prayers.

Billy's picture on his tombstone is chipped and cracked now after years of being exposed to the elements, but the words of scripture will never fade.

Like Billy's soul, they *will never pass away.*

Bibliography

James W. Bruce III. *From Grief to Glory: Spiritual Journeys of Mourning Parents.* Copyright 2002 by Crossway Books a division of Good News Publishers, Prologue page 16.
http://www.grieftoglory.com/prologue.html>

Larry Woody. *A Dixie Farewell: The Life and Death of Chucky Mullins.* Copyright 1993, Eggman Publishing.
http://www.getcited.org/pub/100177641

Pittsburgh PostGazette.com: Front Page Thursday, June 19, 2003.
http://www.post-gazette.com/

Pittsburgh PostGazette.com: June 20, 2003
http://www.post-gazette.com/sports/pitt/20030620pittfallspitt1.asp

Pittsburgh Tribune June 19, 2003
http://www.pittsburghlive.com/x/pittsburghtrib/s_140634.html

Pittsburgh Tribune June 20, 2003
http://www.pittsburghlive.com/x/pittsburghtrib/s_140835.html

Pittsburgh PostGazette.com: June 19, 2003
http://www.post-gazette.com/sports/pitt/20030619gainessppitt1.asp

Pittsburgh PostGazette.com: September 21, 2003
http://www.post-gazette.com/localnews/20030921krawczyk0921p3.asp

BLOOD on a Pew

Pittsburgh Tribune October 2, 2003
http://www.pittsburghlive.com/x/pittsburghtrib/s_157893.html

Pittsburgh Tribune June 20, 2003
http://www.pittsburghlive.com/x/pittsburghtrib/s_140835.html

Pittsburgh Tribune June 29, 2003
http://www.pittsburghlive.com/x/pittsburghtrib/s_142296.html

Pittsburgh PostGazette.com: June 27, 2003
http://www.post-gazette.com/sports/columnists/20030627shelly.asp

Pittsburgh Tribune June 22, 2003
http://www.pittsburghlive.com/x/pittsburghtrib/s_141128.html

Pittsburgh PostGazette.com: November 14, 2004
http://www.post-gazette.com/pg/04319/411732.stm

Pittsburgh Tribune August 24, 2003
http://www.pittsburghlive.com/x/pittsburghtrib/s_151505.html

Orlando Sentinel September 12, 2004
http://www.jonentine.com/reviews/Orlando_01.htm

Pittsburgh Tribune June 19, 2003
http://www.pittsburghlive.com/x/pittsburghtrib/s_140693.html

Pittsburgh PostGazette.com: October 11, 2002
http://www.post-gazette.com/sports/pitt/20021011pittpitt3p3.asp
http://recruiting.scout.com/2/11087.html
http://footballrecruiting.rivals.com/
http://www.usatoday.com/sports/college/football/
bigeast/2003-08-10-pitt-fitzgerald_x.htm

Bruce Feldman. ESPN Magazine. August 2001.
Article on recruitment of Marcus Vick.

Pittsburgh PostGazette.com: June 27, 2003
http://www.post-gazette.com/localnews/20030627priestreg4p4.asp

Bibliography

Pittsburgh PostGazette.com: June 28, 2003
http://www.post-gazette.com/forum/20030628edgaines0628p2.asp

Pittsburgh Tribune June 21, 2003
http://www.pittsburghlive.com/x/pittsburghtrib/s_141098.html

Pittsburgh PostGazette.com: July 8, 2003
http://www.post-gazette.com/localnews/20030708priest0708p3.asp

Pittsburgh Tribune June 26, 2003
http://www.pittsburghlive.com/x/pittsburghtrib/s_141679.html

Pittsburgh Tribune June 25, 2003
http://www.pittsburghlive.com/x/pittsburghtrib/s_141513.html

Pittsburgh Tribune June 25, 2003
http://www.pittsburghlive.com/x/pittsburghtrib/s_141476.html

Pittsburgh Tribune June 24, 2003
http://www.pittsburghlive.com/x/pittsburghtrib/s_141381.html

Pittsburgh Tribune June 22, 2003
http://www.pittsburghlive.com/x/pittsburghtrib/s_141202.html

Pittsburgh Tribune September 25, 2003
http://www.pittsburghlive.com/x/pittsburghtrib/s_156768.html

Pittsburgh Tribune August 28, 2003
http://www.pittsburghlive.com/x/pittsburghtrib/news/s_152159.html

Pittsburgh Tribune March 17, 2003
http://www.pittsburghlive.com/x/pittsburghtrib/s_184899.html

Pittsburgh Tribune June 23, 2003
http://www.pittsburghlive.com/x/pittsburghtrib/s_141264.html

Pittsburgh Tribune August 27, 2003
http://www.pittsburghlive.com/x/pittsburghtrib/s_151988.html

Pittsburgh Tribune September 23, 2003
http://www.pittsburghlive.com/x/pittsburghtrib/s_156387.html

BLOOD on a Pew

Pittsburgh Tribune September 9, 2003
http://www.pittsburghlive.com/x/pittsburghtrib/news/s_154044.html

Pittsburgh Tribune July 12, 2003
http://www.pittsburghlive.com/x/pittsburghtrib/news/s_144297.html

WBAL TV Channel 11. January 10, 2006
http://www.wbaltv.com/news/5989130/detail.html

Pittsburgh Tribune June 25, 2003
http://www.pittsburghlive.com/x/pittsburghtrib/s_141513.html

C.S. Lewis. *The Screwtape Letters.* Copyright 1942, C. S.Lewis Pte. Ltd. Copyright restored 1996 C. S. Lewis Pte. Ltd.